Islam

Architect of a Progressive Civilization

Dr. Shah Ebadur Rahman Neshat

Former professor of English
Umm al-Qura University, Makkah

Published by

Abul Hasan Ali Nadwi Study Circle

H-14, Abul Fazl Enclave, Jamia Nagar, Okhla

New Delhi 110025, India

drserahman@gmail.com

Year of Publication: 2020 (first edition)

Dedicated to

my maternal uncle and aunt
(mamoo and mamani)

Dr. S. M. Zakiuddin and Bibi Nasima Khatoon
(May Allah bless them with paradise!)

Contents

FOREWORD

A new allegation against Islam is in the air nowadays. It is said that Islam is incompatible with the ideology of progress and is therefore a misfit in the modern world. Graham E. Fuller mentions it with his stricture in these words: "What is most disturbing is that we now face quite extraordinary remarks from the entire class of right-wing ideologists who actually challenge the fundamental *humanity* of Muslims – as products of a culture that is *fundamentally incapable of joining global civilization* – as if Islam had had no major part in creating it."[1]

Recently, in September 2018, a book entitled Feindliche Uber nahme – wie der Islam den Fortschritt und die Gesellschaft bedroht (Hostile Takeover: How Islam Impairs Progress and Threatens Society) has been published in Germany (Kindle, 2018) reiterating this allegation in a full-volume work. The author Thilo Sarazin, an avowed critic of Islam, has argued in his book that Islam is anti-progress. This book has been severely criticized for being based on half-truths and lies, to the extent that a reviewer calls the readers "not to read it." The publication of this book, however, asserts that the critics of Islam are seriously trying to sell this idea.

---

[1] Graham E. Fuller, *A World without Islam* (New York: Back Bay Books: Little, Brown and Company, 2010), p. 232.

We will refute this allegation in the present book and try to establish that Islam is inherently a progressive religion fully capable of leading mankind to peace, prosperity and civilizational excellence. We will show that it has, in fact, done it with full glory only in the recent past which remains a bright chapter in the history of human civilization.

Shah Ebadur Rahman Neshat

Delhi, December 31, 2018

In the name of Allah, Most Beneficent, Most Merciful

INTRODUCTION

Islam as religion is of course mainly concerned with the Hereafter, but it does not denigrate this-worldly engagements as profane. Contrary to it, it exhorts Muslims to play an active role for making the earth an ideal haven for all and promises heavenly rewards if they execute this divine mission sincerely and efficaciously.

That is why, Muslims always took much interest in the progress and prosperity of the lands that they inhabited or ruled, and developed a civilization of their own that promoted, in addition to its moral and spiritual values, material felicity and advancement in all spheres of human society. It is the latter aspect of Islamic civilization that we will try to explore in this book.

We will show in this work that Muslims developed a great empire and a progressive and prosperous civilization at the global level only in the recent past which remains a glorious chapter in the history of civilization and proves beyond doubt Muslims' capacity to lead humankind to prosperity.

As it is not feasible to cover the diverse achievements of Muslims in a short work like this, we will limit the discussion to only three prominent areas and consider them as indicators of Muslims' achievements in other fields as well. These three areas are: (1) establishment of a large Islamic Empire known for prosperity and progress, (2) key role played by Muslims in creating the European Renaissance, and (3) leadership of Muslims in the creation of modern science. These three areas will be discussed in the same order, with the exception that in the beginning we will add a brief discussion of the Islamic teachings that prepared Muslims for this task. At the end, we will emphasize the natural conclusion of the discussion that what Muslims did in the past under the inspiration of Islam, they could do it in the future as well.

(I)

ISLAMIC GUIDELINES FOR THE FORMATION OF AN IDEAL CULTURE

In this section we will take a look at some prominent Islamic teachings which prepared Muslims to establish progress, prosperity and peace on earth, as a result of which virtue prevailed, egalitarianism was established and injustice was reduced to the minimum.

1. ONENESS OF GOD (TAWHID)

Tawhid, or Oneness of God, was the foremost tenet of Islamic creed enjoining upon humans that they worship Him alone and offer total submission to Him. This faith in God as being the only deity, the absolute master of the earth and the heavens, helped Muslims rise above the fear that anything other than God could ever influence their destiny. They were thus armed with a faith that equipped them with courage, confidence and ambition necessary to overcome hurdles and initiate the process of establishing a quality human society on earth. Philip K. Hitti acknowledged this fact in these words: "In this uncompromising monotheism, with its simple, enthusiastic faith in the supreme rule of a transcendent being, lies the chief strength of Islam as a religion. Its adherents enjoy a contentment and resignation unknown among followers of other creeds. Suicide is rare in Muslim lands."[2] He wrote further: "As for the Arabians [read 'Muslims'] themselves, they represented a fresh and vigorous stock fired with new enthusiasm, imbued with the will to conquer and emboldened by the utter contempt of death inculcated by their new faith."[3]

2. MAN, GOD'S VICEGERENT ON EARTH

Islam taught that man was appointed by God as the caretaker of the earth (Quran 2: 30) and was given the responsibility of running it in the best interest of humankind in accordance with God's instructions. This was a religious duty for which he was answerable to God. He deserved rewards if he fared well and risked punishment if he failed. In order to help him fulfil this mission efficiently, God inculcated "reason" and "benevolence" in his nature so that he could plan rationally and execute his plans benevolently for the benefit of humans. Muslims were also responsible for preserving ecological balance of nature and for protecting animals, birds and beasts, plants and trees, seas and mountains, and life in different forms.

---

[2] Philip K. Hitti, *The Arabs: A Short History* (Washington D. C.: Regnery Publishing, 1970), p. 48.
[3] Hitti, pp. 57-58.

3. IMPORTANCE OF KNOWLEDGE

The importance attached to knowledge in Islam was manifest in the fact that the first word of the first revelation in Islam was *iqra*, which meant "read." Islam thus urged its adherents from the very beginning to acquire knowledge, which had to be their special qualification so as to help them exploit worldly resources for the benefit of humankind. The five verses revealed on this occasion to Prophet Muhammad, peace be upon him, who was unlettered and lived in a virtually illiterate community, were loaded with topics belonging to the realm of science, of which the Makkans of the time could make neither the head nor the tail. These verses mentioned Allah as one "Who created man from the clot of blood," "Who taught mankind by pen," and taught mankind "to acquire knowledge hitherto unknown to them through pen" (Quran 2: 1-5). The Quran reinforced the importance of knowledge by teaching Muslims the supplication: "Lord! Increase me in knowledge" (Quran 20: 114). And still further, it urged Muslims to rise above the level of merely reading and writing and concentrate on *pondering* and *reflecting* (*tadabbur*) on the signs in nature in order to comprehend the omniscience, omnipresence and omnipotence of God. In addition, Islam connected knowledge to "practice" by clarifying that Muslims would be able to create "a good human society" on earth only when they practice what they profess. Thus prepared, Muslims looked at life with a vision that the learned and the ignorant could not be equal.

4. ALL HUMANS ARE EQUAL

In Islam, none was superior to others on the basis of gender, race, color or nationality. Humans were the progeny of Adam and were thus equals, in fact, relatives. Islam granted the same status to converts that the born Muslims enjoyed, regardless of the fact that a convert in question was an Arab or a non-Arab, a male or a female, a tribal chief or a slave. In the same way, Islam allotted a prestigious position to non-Muslims in an Islamic state and ensured full protection to their individual, social and religious rights. Islam carved out full provision for them to freely practice their religion in an Islamic state and live by their own religious Personal Law. It was acknowledged that if a non-Muslim resident of an Islamic state ever felt that his right was violated, he was fully entitled to sue the offender in an Islamic court, even if the alleged offender was the Head of the Islamic state.[4] Thus Islam forged men and women from different backgrounds into a closely-knit community. Philip K. Hitti acknowledges it in these words: "In this period of unprecedented expansion, the Muslim Arabs 'assimilated' to their creed, speech and even physical type, more aliens than any stock before or since, not excepting the Hellenic, the Roman, the Anglo-Saxon or the Russian."[5]

---

[4] The Prophet is reported to have said that if a non-Muslim resident of an Islamic state was unjustly hurt by a Muslim, the Prophet himself would plead for the non-Muslim sufferer against the Muslim offender on the Day of Judgment.

[5] Hitti, p. 1.

5. ISLAMIC SHARIAH: ITS CONTEMPORANEITY AND COMPREHENSIVENESS

The Islamic *Shariah,* a set of legal directives, provided guidance to Muslims regarding their conduct in all spheres of life. Its comprehensiveness relieved Muslims from the obligation of drawing from scratch an appropriate law for doing or not doing a deed: the legal directives regarding all deeds and situations were already provided. If there ever arose a new issue, the parameters were there to sort it out in consonance with Islamic Law.

The legal framework that Muslim scholars developed in order to find out an Islamic solution to a new issue was fully rational and satisfied all demands of contemporaneity and practicality. In such a situation they 1) consulted the Quran for guidance, but if not finding an adequate guideline there, they 2) went to hadith. If not fully satisfied there either, they looked for 3) a relevant and reliable "precedent" in the early history of Islam which could be the basis of a general consensus among Muslim scholars of the time. But if even that did not work, they, 4) finally, took resort to individual conjecture (*qiyaas*), which meant that a scholar employed his best intellectual ability, understanding of Islamic Shariah, and *taqwa* (fear of God) to decide what verdict was most appropriate on the issue concerned.

6. THE ARABIC LANGUAGE

Initially, Arabic was just a regional language, but after the emergence of Islam, it successfully fulfilled its new responsibilities and soon assumed a global character. As Hitti writes: "In the meantime it had established itself as the language of diplomacy and polite intercourse from Central Asia, through the whole length of Northern Africa, to Spain. Since that time the people of Iraq, Syria and Palestine as well as of Egypt, Tunisia, Algeria and Morocco have expressed their best thought in the tongue of the Arabians."[6] Since Arabic was the language of the Quran and Hadith and since Muslims offered their obligatory prayers in Arabic five times a day, the believers were naturally bound by a common linguistic tie which helped them minimize their geographical and cultural differences and prejudices.

The Islamic teachings discussed above enlightened, prepared and urged Muslims to march on the path of progress and prosperity, as a result of which they were able to create a civilization of their own which is remembered in history for its glory and grandeur.

---

[6] Hitti, p. 121.

(II)

PROSPERITY AND PROGRESS UNDER THE MUSLIM RULE

INTRODUCTION

Islam grew through its evolutionary stages step by step – from a faith to a society, to a culture, to a state, to a civilization. The Prophet of Islam got twenty-three years in all for preaching his message, but in this short period he established Islam in the whole of the then Arabia. And then in less than a century his followers formed a large empire covering three sub-continents – Asia, Africa and Europe. Philip K. Hitti acknowledges it in these words: "One hundred years after the death of Muhammad his followers were the masters of an empire greater than that of Rome at its zenith, an empire extending from the Bay of Biscay to the Indus and the confines of China and from the Aral Sea to the lower cataracts of the Nile. The name of the prophet-son of Arabia, joined with the name of Almighty Allah, was being called five times a day from thousands of minarets scattered over southwestern Europe, northern Africa and western and central Asia."[7]

This rapid spread of Islam cannot be explained in terms of Muslims' numerical superiority (for in most encounters they were less in number than their enemies), war techniques (for they were familiar with only tribal war techniques), or superiority of arms (for their arms were surely inferior to those of the Persians and Romans). Hitti acknowledges the role of Islam's spiritual appeal in its success. He writes: "The strength of the Moslem Arabian army lay neither in the superiority of its arms nor in the excellence of its organization but in its higher morale, to which religion undoubtedly contributed its share?"[8] The shift of political power from the Roman and Persian centers to the Muslim hands seemed such an impossibility in the first third of the seventh century that whoever would have dared to prophesy it, "he would have been declared a lunatic."[9]

But Muslims achieved this unexpected success nevertheless, and then they achieved even a greater success: they introduced a high-level prosperity in the lands that had fallen under their control. In addition, they generously shared the fruits of their success with all, Muslims as well as non-Muslims.

In order to show how Muslims achieved this remarkable success, we will establish a historical framework.

---

[7] Hitti, p. 1.
[8] Hitti, p. 59.
[9] Hitti, p. 56.

We will begin with the Prophet's Age and see how the Islamic principles guaranteeing the formation of a healthy and just society were first laid down in the lifetime of the Prophet. We will then take a look at how a state based on the teachings of Islam emerged during the period of the first four caliphs known as "the Rightly-guided Caliphs" (*Kholafāe Rashidin*). After that we will discuss the remarkable prosperity and progress achieved during the four Muslim caliphates – the Umayyads, the Abbasids, the Fatimids and the Muslim state of Spain – which followed immediately after the rule of the Rightly-guided Caliphs. This framework will oblige us to cover a hundred years' history of the Muslims, which, though a little long for this short work, should sufficiently reveal the inclinations and preferences of Muslims at different times and climes.

A. THE PROPHET'S AGE (623-632 AD)

As we intend to investigate the status of progress and prosperity during the age of the Prophet, we will deal with the Madinan period only, for the essential features of Islamic civilization, which bloomed in later years, were laid down first in this very period.

1. Messenger of Peace and Goodwill

The Prophet's preferences and priorities in what he did after reaching Madinah clearly reflect that his ambitions were out and out positive and noble. A brief appraisal of his actions below will provide us with an insight into the principles on which he founded the Muslim community there.

a) As the Prophet of Allah was entrusted with the divine duty to establish a society on earth which could help human beings connect to their Creator with right belief and good actions, he did two things after arriving in Madinah. He first constructed a mosque to establish five-time prayers there, and then built a platform attached to it called *Suffa* to instruct Muslims in religion. This way the believers were connected to their Prophet for learning the religion of Islam and practicing the religious duties under his guidance.

b) The Prophet established between the *Muhājirin* (the Migrants from Makkah) and the *Ansār* (the Helpers from Madinah) a new bond of brotherhood by picking up suitable couples, one from each of the two groups, and declaring them as brothers in religion, although they had no blood or tribal relationship. Thus, the traditional prominence of tribal bond was done away with and in its place was established a religious relationship, which was to emerge later as a universal Islamic value. It was done in history at such a large scale for the first time. The Ansār gave the Muhājirin an equal share in their residence and property and took the relationship of Islamic brotherhood to a height unknown to humanity, before or since.

c) The Prophet initiated and entered into a peace treaty with the Jews residing in and around Madinah, Banu Nadīr, Banu Qurayza and Banu Qaynuqa', in order to promote the principle of peaceful co-existence with non-Muslims. R. V. C. Bodley informs us about the terms of the treaty in these words: "The Jews who attach themselves to our commonwealth shall have an equal right with our own people to our assistance and good offices. The Jews of the various branches domiciled in yathrib [Madinah] shall form with the Moslems one composite nation. They shall practice their religion as freely as the Moslems. The clients and allies of the Jews shall enjoy the same security and freedom."[10]

d) The Prophet also signed a peace treaty with the Christians during his Tabuk campaign and with the Christians of Najran with the same religious magnanimity. Mahmudul Hasan Siddiqui and Chiragh Hasan Hasrat document one of his treaties with the Christians in the following words:

---

[10] R. C. V Bodley, *The Messenger: The Life of Muhammad* (New York, Doubleday & Co., 1946), pp. 167-68.

No illegitimate tax shall be imposed on the Christians, no Bishop shall be removed from his official position, no Christian shall be forced to accept Islam, no monk shall be turned out of his monastery, no Christian pilgrim shall be denied the right to visit his religious places, and no church or monastery shall be demolished to create a space for the construction of a mosque or living quarters for Muslims. The Christian ladies entering into marriage with Muslims by their free will shall not be forced to accept Islam; they shall have full freedom to follow their religion [in the houses of their Muslim husbands].[11]

e) The Prophet signed the peace treaty of Hudaybia with the Quraysh by accepting their terms and conditions which were unjust, even humiliating, and initiated a period of peace in the area.

f) He observed full restraint at the time of the conquest of Makkah and declared amnesty for all, including his worst enemies and torturers, discarding the tradition of vengeance and introducing a new war etiquette. As Karen Armstrong acknowledges, "Muhammad [pbuh] took Makkah without shedding a drop of blood…. None of the Quraysh was forced to become Muslims…. Single-handedly, Muhammad [pbuh] had brought peace to war-torn Arabia."[12]

---

[11] Mahmudul Hasan Siddiqui and Chiragh Hasan Hasrat, *Taarekhe Islam* (Urdu), (Karachi: Silver Burdett, 1953), pp. 43-44.

g) And he declared Madinah a *haram,* as Makkah was. Maulana Taqi Usmani writes about the sanctity of *haram* in Islam in these words: "Here [in a *haram*] neither a human being will be killed, nor a battle will be fought (unless there is an emergency), nor an animal will be hunted or cruelly confined to a place. Thus a *haram* is a place of safety and security not only for humans; it is so for animals as well."[13] Those accusing Islam of violence might ask themselves why the Prophet, who was under no obligation to do so, declared Madinah, the capital of the Islamic state, as *haram* (not a military base). This should be remembered that since then Madinah has retained the status of a *haram,* an epitome of peace, to this day.[14]

2. Creation of a New Culture in Madinah

During his ten-year sojourn in Madinah, Prophet Muhammad, blessings and peace be upon him, had to fight several battles

---

[12] Karen Armstrong, *Islam: A Short History* (London: Phoenix, 2002), p. 20.

[13] Taqi Uthmani (Maulana), *Tawdhi'ul Qur`an* (Urdu), (Deoband: Maktaba Yusufiya, n. y.), p. 80, footnote 81.

[14] The Statue of Liberty in New York is surely a symbol of a nation's wish to uphold *liberty* as its cherished ideal, which should be fully appreciated, but the declaration of Madinah as *haram* by Prophet Muhammad, centuries before the Statue of Liberty was erected, is never mentioned in history as Muslims' effort to establish peace as a religious value.

with the Quraysh, the Jews and the Romans, but his main focus remained on teaching Islam, explicating its tenets and implementing its directives at the individual and social level. We will present below the principles on which he founded the Muslim society at Madinah.

The "political" structure of the society was formed on the principle that Allah was supreme and that Muslims had to conduct all their affairs, personal and collective, in accordance with His directives. A Muslim state was intended to work as a welfare state. A healthy balance was established between the rights and duties of the individual and the state.

The "economic" base of the society was laid down on the principle that richness and poverty in society were deliberately created by the divine will to test mankind in life and watch who is obedient and virtuous (Quran 67: 2). Thus, the rich were supposed to be kind and helpful to the poor, whereas the poor had to demonstrate self-respect and try to fulfill their needs by their own efforts as best as possible. Rich Muslims were encouraged to spend generously to help the needy; hoarding of wealth was discouraged to the maximum so as to promote healthy circulation of money in society.

"Equality of human beings" was strongly emphasized and superiority of one to the other on the basis of color, race, nationality and gender was unequivocally rejected. It was established that all humans were the progeny of Adam, peace be upon him, and that the only thing that could qualify a person as superior to others was piety and benevolence.

The fundamental "moral" principle of Islam was contained in the directive that virtue and moral uprightness would be adopted and vice and transgression of all kinds would be renounced in personal life as much as possible.

The "social" guidelines required that blood relationships, social ties, and human obligations would be duly honored and fulfilled. In matters of right, Muslims would sacrifice their claims as much as possible, but in terms of duty they would always try to fulfill their obligations. In other words, they would try to be duty-conscious instead of right-oriented. Islam laid down the principle that Muslims would help each other in just and virtuous deeds and would never help each other in matters of injustice and oppression. Islam made it obligatory for Muslims to stop each other from indulging in any unjust and tyrannical act (Quran 5: 2). To be kind to the aged, the sick, the widow, the orphan, the traveler and the neighbor was declared as a good deed to be observed by all Muslims.

"Women" were granted a prestigious position in society. Their rights were acknowledged, codified and established at the social level. Muslims were taught that paradise was under the feet of the mother, that putting food in the mouth of wife as a token of indulgence was a virtue ensuring the husband heavenly reward, and that raising a daughter properly, educating her adequately and then marrying her off ensured parents a place in the neighborhood of the Prophet in paradise. A woman was given the right to accept or reject a proposal for marriage, seek separation from her husband if she was not satisfied (called *khula'* in Islamic terminology) and remarry if she so liked. A woman was also given the right of inheritance in the property of her parents and husband. Her right to education, proper employment and conducting an independent business was acknowledged and established.

"Crimes" were declared as punishable by law. Drinking, gambling, professions of immodesty, and immoral acts were banned. Disgust for vice, injustice and oppression of all kinds was created in the individual as well as in the society, as a result of which crimes were reduced to the minimum.

"The rights of non-Muslims" were acknowledged and observed by allowing them to live in an Islamic state with prestige and full religious freedom. The Prophet signed peace treaties with the Jews, the Christians and the polytheist Quraysh on fair terms and kept his word to the last.

Laws were made relating to "war and peace," with emphasis on peace. It was strictly forbidden to kill a woman, a minor, an old person, a monk, or a person who stayed inside his house refusing to fight against Muslims. Muslims were forbidden from killing an enemy in a war who fell injured, or fled the battlefield, or sought peace. It was declared that an envoy should never be slayed so that the door for negotiation remained open and peace was given a chance.[15]

---

[15] For a detailed discussion, see *Was Islam Spread by Sword?* by Dr. Shah

"Rights of animals, birds and insects" were acknowledged and killing them in sport or slaughtering an animal mercilessly was declared un-Islamic. To deny "others" access to a water resource even in a war was forbidden.

To disturb ecological balance in any form was greatly discouraged. It was declared illegal to unnecessarily fell trees or destroy shrubs and plants.

Education was emphasized at all levels. Teaching and learning of Islamic knowledge was adopted as a necessary component of the emerging society. Acquiring useful worldly knowledge was duly appreciated and encouraged.[16] The Prophet had fixed a separate day for women to instruct them in religion.

Proper use of literature, especially poetry, was duly acknowledged. People recited suitable verses of famous Arab poets in the presence of the Prophet and he expressed his appreciation for them. Hassaan bin Thabit was known in the society as the poet of Islam.

On the foundation of the above Islamic teachings there came into existence a society in Madinah which upheld the norms of justice, security and inclusiveness. This society soon

---

Ebadur Rahman Neshat, (New Delhi: Abul Hasan Ali Nadwi Study Circle, 2016).

[16] He asked Zayd bin Haritha to learn the Hebrew language from the Jews and arranged for the Madinan children to learn reading and writing from the prisoners of Badr. He also asked a lady tutor to teach Hafsa®, his wife, to read and write.

evolved into a state so as to manage its expanding societal obligations. This feature started becoming clear in the days of the Rightly-Guided Caliphs - Abu Bakr, Omar, Uthman and Ali, may Allah be pleased with them. How did it happen? This is the subject of the coming section.

B. PERIOD OF THE RIGHTLY-GUIDED CALIPHS (632-661 A.D.)

After the death of Prophet Muhammad, the task of preserving and promoting the message of Islam fell on the shoulders of his Companions. Muslim historians agree that the first four caliphs were so successful in keeping the form and spirit of the teachings of the Prophet that they were given the title of "the Rightly-guided Caliphs" (*Khulafāe Rāshidin*). We will discuss below their contributions individually, one by one, so as to assess how the period of each of them was marked by progress, prosperity and justice.

1. Abu Bakr (632-634 AD)

Abu Bakr, the first caliph, was elected by consensus in an open meeting of the Muhājirin and Ansār, which was finally authenticated by the Muslim mass in the form of an oath of allegiance (*bai'ah*) offered to him. We will quote below a portion from his first address to Muslims in order to show what the caliphate actually means in Islam.

> I am appointed as your chief, although I am not the best among you. Therefore, support me if I perform rightly, and rectify me if I go wrong.... By the will of Allah, a weak person among you is strong in my sight so that I secure his right, and a strong person among you is weak in my sight so that I retrieve from him the rightful claim of others.... Obey me as long as I obey Allah and the Prophet, but if I disobey them, you do not owe obedience to me.[17]

The period of Abu Bakr's caliphate was full of challenges for the newborn state of Madinah. Several of the neighboring tribes who had professed Islam turned insurgent: some declined to pay *Zakah* (poor due), which was a fundamental tenet of Islam, while a few opportunists declared themselves as messengers of God and by gathering followers from their tribes threatened the security of Madinah. At that time this question assumed great importance whether the army of Osama bin Zayd, which was dispatched by the Prophet himself to march toward Syria and was now waiting outside the city

---

[17] Shah Moinullah Nadwi, Siyarus Sahabah, vol. 1, (Lahore: Idara Islamiyaat, n.y), p. 41-42. Translation from Urdu to English here and elsewhere is mine.

for new orders in face of the sudden death of the Prophet, should be allowed to proceed to Syria or be held at Madinah to defend it in case of an attack from the enemies.

Abu Bakr® ordered Osama to proceed to Syria, asserting that he would not revoke a command of the Prophet, whatever the odds. He himself went out of Madinah to send Osama off and gave him instructions on that occasion that truly revealed what rules of war he had inherited from the Prophet of Allah. Needless to say that those very rules remained valid for ever for Muslims. He instructed Osama in particular and Muslim soldiers in general in these words:

> Muslims! Raise your sword against those only who raise their swords against you. Fight only those who fight you. Make sure that you do not attack women, children and the old; instead, treat them with courtesy and kindness. Do not hurt those [the non-Muslim monks] who restrict themselves in monasteries for worshipping God according to their faith. Destroy the harvest not, nor fell trees.[18]

After that he sent a clear and strong message to the rebellious tribes which wanted to remain Muslim without paying zakat and made it clear to them that Islam was what the Prophet had taught and that its fundamentals could not be ever changed under any willful pressure. This nipped the uprising in the bud.

---

[18] Siddiqui and Hasrat, p. 58.

Then he challenged the false prophets and by defeating one in the battlefield and demoralizing the other by military maneuvers put this threat to the integrity of Islam and to the security of Madinah to an end.

But by this time the governors of the Persian Empire in Iraq and of the Romans in Syria increased their hostile military maneuvers against Muslims on the borders. The Persians, who were fire-worshippers, and the Romans, who were Christians, considered the rise of Islam as detrimental to their interest and wished to eliminate it as early as possible. Sure enough, Muslims were not a match to them in number or military might. In addition, Muslims had not yet recovered from the shock of the death of their Prophet. But, in face of the incursion of the Roman and Persian governors on the Muslim borders, Abu Bakr had no option except to put his resources together and get ready to face the situation.

Confrontation with Persia began first. Muslims defeated the allies of Persia on the border of Arabia, and then marched on Iraq, which was a part of the Persian Empire. Khalid bin Walid was in command. The Muslims conquered Iraq.

But at that time the Arab tribe of Ghassān which ruled a large area on the border of Arabia in the name of the Roman emperor began to attack Muslim borders. This compelled Muslims to fight at two different fronts. Their situation was so precarious that when they decided to face the Romans in Syria, they had to ask Khalid bin Walid, their only trusted military commander at that time, to leave Iraq, where he was fighting the Persians, and rush to take charge of the Syrian front against the Romans. The situation was against the Muslims, but they won the battle. They also defeated the Romans in the battle of Ajnādayn, where the Romans had brought a huge army against them. The Roman emperor escaped to Antioch. That was the time when Abu Bakr® died in Madinah.

Abu Bakr ruled for about two years only in which he had to fight against local insurgents, the Persians, and the Romans, but in this short and turbulent period he very ably strengthened Islam and organized Muslims. He closed the doors forever to the possibility of allowing under pressure any change in the fundamentals of Islam. He also collected the whole Quran in one volume, established authentic teachings of Islam in the society and organized the affairs of the Islamic state strictly on the lines of the Shariah. He worked day and night to ensure that people lived in peace and security and that justice prevailed in the society. His impeccable character served for all as a model of piety and sincerity. Although he had discontinued his personal business in order to manage state affairs and lived on a meager stipend from the public treasury, he at the time of his death instructed his family members to sell his personal property and return to the treasury (*Baytul Maal*) all the money that he had received as stipend.

2. Omar bin Khattaab (634-644 AD)

Omar ibn Khattaab®, the second caliph in Islam, also chose to tread in the footsteps of the Prophet by following the precedent of Abu Bakr. He lived a life of austerity and never wavered in administering justice in the land. When he became the caliph, Muslims were already fighting against the Persians and the Romans. He had thus inherited a situation that he could not escape. All he could do was to organize his resources and face the enemies.

He first concentrated at the Syrian front against the Romans. Muslims captured Damascus, the capital of Syria. The Roman emperor Heraclius tried to take it back and challenged Muslims in the battlefield of Yarmouk with an army of two-hundred thousand soldiers. Muslims were thirty to forty thousand only, but they inflicted a decisive defeat on the Romans and ended the rule of Rome in Syria forever.[19]

---

[19] Two incidents relating to *jizya* are worth mentioning here. When the Roman king Heraclius proceeded toward Syria to attack Muslims, Muslims strategically vacated Syrian cities like Damascus and Homs in order to assemble their entire military strength at one point to be able to fight the Romans better. While vacating the cities under their control, they returned the jizya money to the non-Muslim residents telling them that as they were now not in a position to protect them against the invading Roman army, they had to, according to the Islamic law, refund the Jizya money which was taken from them for guaranteeing their safety from internal disturbances and outside enemies. And second, when Muslims besieged the city of Jarjouma, a Roman city, the residents thereof wanted to make peace with them. But they declined to convert to Islam or pay jizya. They, however, agreed that in case of a war, they would fight from the side of the Muslims.

Omar did not want to enter into a war against the Persians. But when the Persian army proceeded toward the Muslim territories in order to take back the areas that it had lost to Muslims, a war between them became imminent. The battle of Qadisiyya was decisive for both the Muslims and the Persians. Rustam, the Persian commander, challenged the Muslims at Qadisiyya with an army of about one-hundred-fifty thousand soldiers, accompanied by a special squad of fighter elephants. The elephants created a havoc among the Muslim soldiers by frightening the horses on the Muslims side. But the Muslims, who were much inferior in number, risked their lives and ultimately defeated the Persians.

Muslims now proceeded toward Ctesiphon (al-Madain) which was the capital of Persia. As it was situated at the bank of the River Tigris, it could be reached only by a bridge. In fact, there was a bridge over it which the Persians had destroyed in order to block the passage for the Muslims. Finding no way out, the Muslim commander Sa'ad bin Waqqās put his horse into the river and started swimming toward al-Madain with the help of his horse. The Muslim soldiers followed their commander and soon they all were in the river swimming

---

Since Muslims collected poll tax (jizya) from their non-Muslim subjects in lieu of the exemption they granted them from participating in a war, Muslims accepted the proposal of the people of Jarjouma and the non-Muslim residents thereof lived in peace and honor there along with their Muslim conquerors without paying any poll tax. (Siddiqui and Hasrat, p.67-68).

toward al-Madain. The Persians had never thought that humans could ever do so. They did not believe their eyes and seeing in it some kind of supernatural element hurriedly vacated al-Madain without resistance. The King Yazdegerd was also with them. The Muslims captured al-Madain and then by subduing neighboring cities took the whole Iraq in control.[20] The Persians tried to take Iraq back and attacked Muslims, but in a decisive battle at Nahavand they suffered a defeat in which the emperor Yazdegerd was killed. Thus the Persian Empire came to an end and the word of the Prophet of Islam turned out to be true that as the Persian ruler had torn in pieces the Prophet's letter sent to him, so would be torn asunder his empire.

As the conquest of Jerusalem holds a special significance in the career of the caliph Omar®, we will allot it here some extra space. When the Christians realized that they could not defend Jerusalem against the invasion of the Muslims, they agreed to surrender provided the caliph Omar would himself come down from Madinah to sign the peace treaty. It was a cumbersome condition and the Muslims did not have to oblige the losing Christians. But as it promised the conquest of Jerusalem without war, the caliph Omar traveled

---

[20] Siddiqui and Hasrat, p. 72. Mohammad Iqbal, the famous poet, has versified this incident in an Urdu couplet, which runs like this: *"Dasht to dasht, na darya bhi hain choRe hamne/bahre zulmaat men dawRa diye ghoRe hamne"* (We've spared neither forests nor rivers/ we plunged our horses in the Black Sea).

to Jerusalem in which he was accompanied only by a slave and had a bag of humble food items to help them at meal times. They had only one camel which both of them rode in turn. When he entered Jerusalem for formal takeover of the city, he walked with the Bishop talking to him in a friendly way. He visited the mosque first and then went to see the church with the Bishop. While still there, the time of Zuhr (Noon) prayer arrived. Courteously, the Bishop suggested that Omar offer his prayers in the church. Omar, nevertheless, walked out of the church and prayed outside. This he did in order to make sure that in future Muslims did not use his praying in the church as a precedent and violate the sanctity of the church.[21] After taking control of Jerusalem he acknowledged the religious rights of the Christians and the Jews to visit and pray in Jerusalem according to their religious traditions, which was practically observed throughout the Muslim rule in Jerusalem.

Soon Egypt was also annexed. The Berbers of Tripoli accepted Islam without any military encounter.[22]

The rule of Omar is known for great administration. State informers were deputed at all important places to keep the caliph posted on what was happening around. Omar himself took night rounds in and around the city of Madinah to keep himself abreast of the needs and inclinations of the Muslims. The Muslim conquests were bringing wealth to the

---

[21] Moinuddin Nadwi, pp. 126-127.
[22] Moinuddin Nadwi, pp. 73-76.

capital, but due to his moral influence the lifestyle of Muslims did not yield to lavishness or lethargy. Individual liberty was so publicly acknowledged that even a common person could question Omar himself and on occasions took him to court. On one occasion he publicly punished the son of the governor of Egypt for unjustly whipping a Coptic Christian: he asked the Christian youth to whip the offender Muslim in the presence of his governor father and after the execution of the punishment admonished the governor in these memorable words: "Since when have you started enslaving people when their mothers had given birth to them as free?" In a murder case, he handed over the Muslim offender to the relatives of the non-Muslim victim who killed him in retaliation. When he reached Jerusalem in order to take the charge of the city, his slave was riding the camel and he was walking on foot as it was then the turn of the slave to ride.

3. Uthman bin 'Affān (644-656 AD)

Uthman bin 'Affān was the third caliph of Muslims. He continued in his office for about twelve years. He was elected as caliph by a high-power committee appointed by the second caliph Omar bin Khattab for this purpose. The general public then stamped their approval by offering an oath of allegiance (*bai'ah*) to him.

In the first six years of his tenure, the Islamic state saw great prosperity. The areas across the River Ceyhan (Jayhun) were annexed and the conquest of Balakh, Hirat, Ghazni and

Kabul took Muslims to the north-west borders of India. Abdullah bin Sa'ad, the governor of Egypt, secured a firm hold on Tripoli and conquered Carthage. Nawbia was also taken. Amir Mu'awiya, governor of Syria, developed a strong navy and by defeating the Roman navy wrenched from them the control of Cyprus and Rhodes Islands.[23]

By now the Muslim Empire had expanded to a very wide area where there were also men who nourished grudge and ill will against Muslims. Such people started spreading misinformation against the caliph in order to weaken the center. Abdullah bin Saba, a Jew from Yemen, was their leader. He gathered a number of followers around him in Kufa and Basra and started working on his mission secretly in a planned way. The caliph came to know about it and called a meeting of the governors to discuss this issue. Remedies were decided upon. But as the places under the influence of the insurgents were far from Madinah and as this work was being carried out underground, it could not be effectively checked. It spread further and reached Egypt. At one point the insurgents gathered in Madinah in the days of Hajj, when most Muslims were in Makkah to perform Hajj, and killed the caliph.

The Caliph Uthman was a trusted Companion of the Prophet and was very dear to him. He had done so many philanthropic works for Muslims by using his personal resources. As caliph, he had taken necessary steps to

---

[23] Siddiqui and Hasrat, pp. 78-79.

popularize the one authentic version of the Quran and made an official announcement that it had to be recited in the dialect of the Quraysh, in which the Prophet used to recite it. During his regime new areas were annexed, borders were guarded and Muslims enjoyed prosperity. When the insurgents assembled in Madinah, he could have eliminated them by using his resources as caliph, but that would have made Muslims fight Muslims. He refused to do so and saved the unity of the Muslim ummah by tacitly accepting his martyrdom.

4. Ali bin Abi Talib (656-661 AD)

Gripped by grief and confusion, the Muslims immediately chose Ali bin Abi Talib as their leader and offered bai'ah at his hands. He thus became the fourth caliph of Islam. Undoubtedly, he was the most appropriate choice, but the challenge in front of him was very difficult and complex. Muslims in general wanted that the killers of Uthman® must be punished befittingly without delay. The difficulty of the newly elected caliph, however, was that the insurgents had gathered enormous power and a rash crackdown on them would have undoubtedly caused a civil war. There was another difficulty: there was no eye-witness of the incident who could identify the criminals.

Ali® first wanted to take the situation in control and then deal with the insurgents, but the agitated Muslim mass was not ready to accept any delay. The situation became very grave when some very respectable Companions, such as Zubayr®, Talha® and *Ummul Momineen* Aisha® also joined the general Muslims demanding immediate action against the insurgents. This divided Muslims into two camps and the situation worsened to the extent that an armed clash could not be avoided. One such battle in which the three above-mentioned Companions faced the Caliph Ali is known as *Ghazwa Jamal* (the Battle of the Camel).

Before the battle ensued, the Caliph Ali tried to negotiate with his opponents. He called Zubayr for a dialogue and reminded him that once when the Prophet had seen Zubayr and Ali walking hand in hand, he had told Zubayr that one day he would fight Ali unjustly.[24] Zubayr recalled the incident. He had come to fight against Ali believing that Ali was wrong, but now he was badly shaken and immediately decided to leave the battlefield. Talha also decided to follow him. This created the prospect of a truce, but a truce would have alienated the murderers of Uthman. They, therefore, waylaid and killed Zubayr and Talha in the way. Ummul Mo`mineen Aisha® also agreed to a truce. The coming morning could have brought peace to Muslims. Realizing that their game could be exposed, the insurgents themselves attacked the army of Ummul Mo`mineen Aisha® in the dark of night and spread misinformation that the army of Ali® had attacked them

---

[24] Moinuddin Nadwi, p. 273.

treacherously. Thus the battle began in which Ali[®] came out victorious.

The Caliph Ali treated Ummul Mo`mineen Aisha with great respect and courtesy. He immediately arranged for her a safe and comfortable residence and allowed her men to stay around her. He himself paid a courtesy visit to her to ensure her of his goodwill. After a talk with Ali which helped her directly listen to his side of the story, she realized that the whole case was maliciously misrepresented and blown up out of all proportion by the insurgents. Graciously, she announced that her differences with Ali were sadly based on gross misunderstanding and that she now took back all her charges against him. Ali on his part made special arrangements for her comfortable stay at Basra for a few days. He then arranged for her journey back to Madinah in such an exemplary way that her brother Muhammad bin Abu Bakr was asked to accompany her, forty ladies of Basra accompanied her in the journey, he himself rode with her caravan to some distance to see her off, and sent his sons to accompany her up to the next stopover.[25]

The difference among Muslims came to an end at this level, but a truce could not be achieved between the Caliph Ali and Amīr Muawiya, the governor of Syria. Amīr Muawiya's claim was that Ali should first arrest and hand over the murderers of Uthman to him while Ali asked him to first offer

---

[25] Moinuddin Nadwi, vol. 1, p. 275.

bai'ah to him as caliph and then raise the case of Uthman's murder. This led to several military encounters between them. As a result, the Muslim power was divided between two camps: Amīr Mu'awiya declared himself ruler of Syria and the Caliph Ali® moved his capital to Kufa in Iraq where he established his rule.

The Caliph Ali was the best model of personal genius and the Prophet's training. He was a very brave person and a very capable ruler. His conduct was a model of piety, his words were the pearls of wisdom and his forbearance was exemplary. His name is dear to Muslims' hearts and inspires them with *taqwa* and *ikhlaas*. His rule was marked by impeccable justice and overall prosperity in the society. He defended the borders of the Islamic state with great success and annexed new lands.

The Period of the Rightly-guided Caliphs: An Overview

This point is crucial and should not be overlooked that the political upheaval did not disturb Islam as religion in anyway. Islam continued to remain the guiding force for Muslims, its tenets fully protected in theory as well as in practice. The disputes that arose among leaders were concerning outer issues. Below we will see how the society, inspired by Islamic spirit, developed a structure which stands as truly modern in all respects by the present-day criteria.

1. The caliph (*khalifa*) was elected by the Muslim mass, which was carried out in different ways. He was elected in an open gathering of Muslims, as was done in the case of Abu Bakr; or he was appointed to this office by the retiring caliph after due consultation with the leaders of the community, as was done in the case of Omar; or he was recommended by a high-power committee formed for this purpose by the retiring caliph, as was done in the case of Uthman; or he was approached by the Muslims themselves to take that position, as was done in the case of Ali. In all situations the Muslim ummah finally stamped their approval by offering an oath of allegiance to him. The chief criterion remained suitability of the candidate, not his lineage. A candidate never put up his name to be considered for the office.

2. The caliph was not a sovereign, free to rule in his own way. Like all other Muslims, he was supposed to follow the rules of the Shariah and manage the affairs of the state by consulting the judicious, sincere and experienced persons from the community. This system was called the *shoura* (the consultative system). When the caliph felt it necessary, he called an open meeting in the mosque and put the matter to the Muslims for open discussion. However, the opinion of the majority was not binding on the caliph. Taking into consideration the interest of Muslims and using his

best discretion, he was the one to take the final decision.

3. The caliph did not enjoy a privileged status on the basis of his office, such as barring a complainant to sue him during his official tenure, or exempting him from appearing in the court to defend a charge against him. A common civilian, a non-Muslim resident of the state, or a humble slave in the society could question him about anything and, if not satisfied, sue him in the court of a *qadi* (the Islamic judge).

4. The judiciary was kept completely free from the influence of the state. If indicted, even the caliph had to appear before the *qadi* to clear his position. The onus of presenting evidence in his support lay on the complainant. Great care was taken to ensure that witnesses were truthful. The *qadi* was given sufficient salary so as to protect him from falling a prey to bribery.

5. As the rule of the land was based on the Shariah, all Muslims were satisfied with it and gladly obeyed it. Thus there existed a healthy balance between the state and the individual minimizing discontent, confusion and exploitation.

6. Islam acknowledged the right of private ownership of property, but it obliged the rich to pay a part of their income as *Zakah* to their poor coreligionists and *sadaqa* (charity) to the needy, whatever their religion. This minimized a clash between the rich and the poor, promoted circulation of money in the interest of the society and discouraged hoarding of wealth. Islam also established law of inheritance, by which it ensured financial stability of the immediate members of the family.

7. The state was responsible to provide basic help to the citizens, especially those who lived below the poverty line. But Islam also encouraged the civilians to do all they could to share their resources with the needy. The tradition of reserving personal property as *waqf* for the welfare of the community is an example of it.

8. The society acknowledged the essential goodness of human beings and accorded them an honorable status. Rights of all – rich and poor, man and woman, free and slave, Muslim and non-Muslim – were fully protected in the light of the teachings of Islam. Slaves were considered as family members and, if they excelled in any appreciable quality, their superiority to free Muslims was openly acknowledged at the social level.[26] All efforts were made to grant them freedom.

9. This whole structure was founded on the teachings of Islam.

C. THE RULE OF THE UMAYYADS (661-750 AD)

The rule of the Umayyad (*khilāfat Banu Umayya*) was founded by Amīr Mu'awiya in 661 A.D. He took Damascus as his capital and ruled over Syria and the adjacent areas. His dynasty ruled for about ninety years.

This period is known for good administration and important conquests. In this period Muslims extended their borders from China to Spain. Muhammad bin Qasim conquered Sindh and Multan in India, Qutayba bin Muslim Bahili pushed forward the boundaries of the Muslim state up to China and Turkistan, and Musa bin Nusayr and Tariq bin Zeyad annexed parts of Africa and Europe. Tariq's conquest of Spain in Europe tells the story of his extraordinary valor. When he landed on Gibraltar with his tiny army consisting of 12,000 soldiers only, he was faced with the opposition of the whole country of Spain, but unintimidated, he ordered his ships to be

---

[26] The high social status of Zayd bin Haritha, Bilal Habashi, Suhayb Rumi, Salman Farsi and many others was a matter of envy even for the tribal chiefs.

set on fire so that his soldiers might not even think of retreating in case of a defeat. This clearly shows that he was fighting for a cause, not for booty or conquering a country to rule over it. In this case chances of Muslims' defeat outweighed those of their success very heavily.[27]

After taking Spain Muslims marched on France and conquered some cities of it. But they were repulsed by the French army under the command of Charles Martel at Tours. They thus could not advance further.

The Umayyads made great strides in different fields. The Muslim navy emerged stronger than the Roman navy and established its control in the sea. They constructed magnificent buildings and built canals to bring water from the sea to the cities for domestic use. In Damascus alone there were seven large canals which supplied water to the houses of the residents, which also helped them develop the culture of

---

[27] Allama Iqbal has versified this historic event in Persian which reads like this:

Tariq chun bar kanarae undlus safeena sokht; guftand kaare tu ba nigahe kherad khataast/ Dooreym az sawaade watan, baaz chun raseym; tarke sabab ze rooe shariat kuja rawaast/ Khandeed, daste kheysh ba shamsheer burdo guft, har mulk mulke mast ke mulke khudaae mast.

(When Tariq set on fire his fleet on the bank of Andalusia; his men told him that his act fell short of wisdom;
Away from our lands, how shall we reach back there?; Is discarding means allowed in shariat?
Tariq softly laughed, put his hand on his sword and said; 'Every country is ours because that is our Lord's.)

keeping backyard gardens, large and small. The Green Palace of Amīr Mu'awiya, the City Mosque of Damascus constructed by the caliph Waleed bin Abdul Malik, and the official palace where the caliph used to hold his court were sites to see. The Arabic language greatly flourished and emerged as the official language of the state. In this period work on the collection of *Hadith* (Traditions of the Prophet) was started. Poetry flourished in this period; Farzdaq and Akhtal were distinguished poets of the time. Islamic jurisprudence (*Fiqh*) also advanced remarkably as a distinguished branch of learning. Imam Abu Haneefa and Imam Malik belonged to this period as did Imam Hasan Basri, Imam Zuhri and Imam Shu'abi. Imam Jafar Sādiq, a descendent of the Prophet known for his exemplary piety, lived in this very period and exerted profound spiritual influence on the people. Omar bin Abdul Azīz ruled for about two years and revived the tradition of the Rightly-guided Caliphs (*Khulafāe Rashidin*).

Muslims also patronized Greek medicine and developed it by performing constant research in the field. This branch of medical science is still flourishing under the patronage of Muslims.[28]

---

[28] It is significant that Muslims have always called it *Tibb Yunani* after the Greeks, and has never shown any desire to give it a Muslim name, although their constant patronage has helped it grow and flourish to this day.

Muslims built new cities to meet the needs of growing population. They also renovated several old cities which were deserted and were now in a dilapidated condition.

Muslims made great advancement in agriculture and gardening. The government encouraged farmers to cultivate unused lands in the state by providing necessary irrigation facilities; it also acknowledged the cultivators' right of ownership over the pieces of land that they cultivated. Muslims also established industries at large and small scales; laws were made for the protection of the rights of laborers. Trades flourished and import and export contacts were established with countries far and near. Mining was developed and important progress was made in this field.

D. THE RULE OF THE ABBASIDS (750 AD-)

After the Umayyads the Abbasids (*Banu Abbas*) came to power. The first caliph of this dynasty was Abul Abbas Abdullah Saffah (750—754 AD). He founded his rule in Damascus and took Anbar as his capital. His brother, Abu Jafar Mansur (754-775 AD), succeeded him and moved his capital to Baghdad.

The Caliph Mansur established an exemplary rule in the country. He abolished bribery from the system, especially from the finance department. Agriculture and trade greatly flourished during his regime. Justice was maintained at an ideal level. Once he appeared in the court of a *qadi* in Madinah under a charge. The *qadi* did not rise to pay him respect; he also gave a verdict against him. Mansur was very pleased to witness the observance of justice in the judiciary.[29] Learning was greatly promoted under Mansur's rule.

Muhammad al-Mahdi (775-785 AD), son of the Caliph Mansur, took over after him. He strove hard to improve public facilities and keep law and order in the state. He started an efficient postal service that connected Madinah, Yemen and Iraq. He also renovated and extended the Prophet's Mosque in Madinah.

Harun al-Rashīd (786-809 AD) was the greatest ruler of this dynasty. He was a religious person and was also a brave and fearless military commander. In most battles he himself commanded his army. The vastness of his empire can be ascertained by what he once said addressing a piece of cloud floating in the sky: "Rain wherever you like, the levy (*khiraaj*) on the harvest watered by you will ultimately come to my coffer." In his reign prosperity was at its apex, but it was not owing to heavy taxation; he achieved it by creating a profitable network of industries, agriculture and trade. John L. Esposito writes: "In a departure from the past, Abbasid success was based not on conquest, but on trade, commerce, industry, and agriculture."[30]

---

[29] Siddiqui and Hasrat, p. 138.

Baghdad, the capital, looked like a magical city. In magnificence and grandeur, it was, in the words of Hitti, "a city with no peer throughout the world."[31] A visitor was captivated by its beauty and majesty, not to mention the specific grandeur of Harun's palace and court. It also had all important government offices in it providing necessary services to citizens. Schools, colleges, mosques, hospitals and inns were there in sufficient number. An offshoot of the Tigris River was diverted to Baghdad which flowed in the midst of the city, supplying water through canals for domestic use. [32]

Harun al-Rashīd was a great patron of learning. Although he ruled in grandeur, he himself used to go to Imam Malik, famous Islamic scholar, to take lessons in Hadith. For translation of important books from other languages, he established a special institution called *Baitul Hikmat* (House of Wisdom). He collected the works of the Greeks that he found during his battles with the Romans, brought them to Baghdad and arranged for their translation into Arabic. Europe came to know and benefit from the works of the Greeks through these very Arabic translations; the original Greek writings were lost long ago.

This point deserves special attention that these Greek books were related neither to Islam nor to Arab culture; some

---

[30] John L. Esposito, *The Straight Path* (New York: Oxford University Press, 1988), p. 58.
[31] Hitti, 110.
[32] Siddiqui and Hasrat, p. 141.

of them even contradicted Islamic teachings. But as Muslims considered knowledge as civilizational inheritance, they protected them, nevertheless. Later, they studied them and registered their agreement or disagreement with them in a purely scholarly spirit.

Women were in general properly educated; many excelled in arts and literature. They participated in social life as well. When the Queen Zubayda, wife of Harun al-Rashīd, came to know that pilgrims to Makkah sometimes died in the days of Hajj due to scarcity of water, she ordered a canal to be constructed to supply water from Tayef to Makkah, a twenty-five mile long project. It is still there and is an architectural wonder in a desert.[33]

The expanse, modernity and splendor of Harun's kingdom was a surprise for Europe. Charlemagne, ruler of France, had sent him a goodwill delegation; Harun had also courteously reciprocated. Charlemagne was at that time the most powerful ruler of the West, but Harun al-Rashīd was "undoubtedly the more powerful and represented the higher culture."[34] Harun had a peace treaty with the Roman emperor Caesar as well. Caesar violated the terms frequently which led to armed confrontation. Harun always won the battle, but he abstained from inflicting harsh punishment on Caesar and never devastated any area of his kingdom.

---

[33] Hitti, p. 111.
[34] Hitti, p. 109.

Mamūn al-Rashīd (813-33 AD), son and successor of Harun al-Rashid, added further grandeur to the Abbasid rule. The Islands of Crete and Sicily were annexed to the Muslim empire during his reign. There was peace and prosperity in the country and the boarders of the state were soundly guarded.

Mamūn was a broad-minded, judicious and brave person. He forgave his worst enemies and ignored the rudeness and intemperance of even his slaves. He bestowed special favors on the learned and scholars and showed no bias against anyone on the basis of religion. On each Tuesday he held a gathering of the distinguished scholars of different religions in his palace in which ideas and opinions were freely exchanged. The caliph participated in the discussion and sat with the scholars down on the carpet.

He took great interest in research, experimentation and invention, especially in the field of science and medicine. In his period a scientist named Abul Hasan invented a telescope. Mamūn constructed an observatory in Baghdad; later such observatories were constructed in other cities as well. He patronized a project to measure the circumference of the earth. He also took personal interest in the activities of *Baitul Hikmah* (House of Wisdom) established by his father Harun al-Rashīd, which prepared and published translations of several important books of past scholars.

The population of Baghdad in the days of Mamūn was two million consisting of people from different races, nationalities and faiths. Muslims and non-Muslims lived together amicably and knew no discrimination.[35]

The Abbasid caliphs ruled for about one hundred years, but when the center became weak, several states broke away and declared themselves independent. Some of them were quite large, like the Samanids and the the Bouehs, and did important developmental work in the lands they ruled. But we cannot discuss them in this short book due to paucity of space.

E. THE RULE OF THE FATIMIDS (909-1171 AD)

After the Abbasids the Fatimids established their caliphate in Egypt, parts of northern Africa, and the islands of Sicily, Sardinia and Corsica in the Mediterranean. At one time all of Syria, Hejaz and a part of Iraq was under the control of a Fatimid caliph named Muizz. The capital of the Fatimids was Cairo, which they had built. The prosperity of the Muslim state can be ascertained by the simple fact that Cairo alone had well over twenty thousand shops to cater the needs of the residents.[36]

---

[35] Siddiqui and Hasrat, pp. 133-150.
[36] Siddiqui and Hasrat, p. 163.

Learning in different fields saw its heyday during the Fatimid rule. Al-Azhar University, a university of international repute to this day, was founded in Egypt in this period. The scientist Alhazen (Ibn al-Haytham), from whom Western scholars like Roger Bacon and Kaplan benefited, belonged to this very period. There were two-hundred thousand (200,000) books in the personal library of one of the Fatimid caliphs, the Caliph Aziz.[37]

The Seljuk took over after the Fatimids and gave the Muslim empire several distinguished rulers. But they mainly deserve a mention here because of a historic service that they rendered to the Muslim nation: they revived the effete institution of the Islamic caliphate. They were Turks from Turkistan who by annexing several small states had carved a fairly large state for themselves. All of Iran, Iraq, the large area between the Tigris and Euphrates, and Minor Asia were under their rule. They then annexed Hejaz, Halab and Turkistan and extended their territories up to the borders of China. Under one of its rulers, Malik Shah (1073-1092 AD) the rule of the Seljuks extended from Kashgar to the Mediterranean islands and from Georgia (Gurjistan) to the Arabian Ocean.

The Seljuk Prime Minister Nizamul Muk Tusi is famous in history for his administration and patronage of learning. He built a great university in Baghdad, Madrasa Nizamiya, an

---

[37] Siddiqui and Hasrat, p. 164.

institution of international repute, which was so prestigious that the most distinguished scholars of the time wished to be among its teaching staff. The famous Islamic scholar Imam Ghazali was its head. Umar Khayyam, the famous poet and scientist, lived in this very period. Jalaluddin Rumi also belonged to this period whose poetry still inspires the East and the West alike with the charm of lyricism and loftiness of thought.

The Zangi dynasty appeared on the scene after the Seljuks. Imaduddin Zangi was valiant, ambitious and good-hearted. If the old, the children and the women were presented to him as prisoners of war, he immediately set them free and returned their property seized as booty. He followed this principle of Islam very strictly: "Fight only those who [initiate] fight with you." He died in the year 1140 A.D.

His son Nuruddin Zangi succeeded him. His life reflected typical piety and reticence that characterized the Companions of the Prophet. He did not take a single penny from the public treasury and supported himself and his family with a meager income from his personal property. In the battle he was always at the forefront. He died in 1174 A.D.

After it the Ayyubi period began. This period is remembered for the crusades in which Sultan Salahuddin Ayyubi played a key role. He conquered Jerusalem in 1187 A.D.

which is considered his greatest achievement in Islamic history. He is famous in Europe for his magnanimity that he displayed in the crusades. He was deeply inspired by the character of the Prophet of Islam. When he conquered Jerusalem, he granted amnesty to all the residents of the city, including the church officials and the soldiers who had fought against him (as the Prophet had done at the conquest of Makkah). He offered the civilians options to live in peace in Jerusalem under the Islamic rule or go to the place of their choice with all their valuables. He also allowed the Christian soldiers who had fought against him to leave the city safely by paying a small ransom (*fidya*). The Sultan himself paid ransom for ten thousand soldiers who could not arrange for money; his brother Malik al-Adil also paid ransom for seven thousand crusaders in order to help them achieve freedom. Thousands of others were freed *gratis*. The Sultan also distributed money among the Christian orphans and widows and arranged transportation for the old and the ailing. Not a single Christian was killed in Jerusalem or in any other city. The right of the Christians and the Jews to visit Jerusalem and perform their religious services there was acknowledged and facilitated as long as the Muslims ruled it.

F. SPAIN: THE UMAYYAD RULE

As mentioned earlier, after conquering Asia and Africa Muslims had entered Europe during the Umayyad period. They had taken Sicily, Crete, Sardinia, Cyprus, Malta and some other Mediterranean islands and established their rule in Spain. They had also annexed a part of France to their territory, entered Italy and moved up to Rome. They had also conquered Provence, Piedmont and Liguria as well as Switzerland. Nice, a famous recreation resort in France, had also fallen to the Muslims. Most of these areas slipped away from the hands of the Muslims with time, but they ruled over Spain, Sicily and Portugal for quite a long time.

With the passage of time the Muslim state in Spain became weak due to civil strife. But In the eighth century the situation changed for Muslims favorably. An Umayyad prince named Abdur Rahman, grandson of the Umayyad Caliph Hisham bin Abdul Malik, reached Spain under special circumstances during the Abbasid period and established his rule there.[38]

Abdur Rahman was a very capable person. He worked day and night to establish himself in Spain and, by rewarding

---

[38] Siddiqui and Hasrat, pp. 216-17.

his supporters generously and developing facilities for the citizens, emerged as an influential force in the area. He built magnificent buildings in Cordova and other cities, dug canals for irrigation and developed agriculture and gardening. The state of Spain became quite strong and prosperous during his reign. He died in 788 A.D.

The death of Abdur Rahman was a setback for the Muslim Spain, but when Abdur Rahman III ascended the throne, he helped Spain regain its past glory. He abolished lawlessness and highway robbery, which had become rampant in the state. He developed agriculture by improving irrigation facilities and utilizing uncultivated lands for agricultural purposes. He also took great interest in gardening: fruit trees – especially those of olive, grape and grapefruit – were cultivated in mountainous expanses. There were olive gardens around the city of Ashbiliya in a very wide area; fruit trees were spread on both sides in Wadi al-Kabir for thirty-seven miles. Industries flourished. Trade with other countries was so prosperous that the government earned 1,20,00000 dinar annually just from duty.

The prosperity enjoyed by the people can be estimated by the fact that in Cordova, the capital of Spain, there were eighty thousand shops, three thousand eight hundred (3,800) mosques and seven hundred public baths providing most modern services, such as hot bath, massage and refreshment. A very high standard was observed in keeping the city clean; a very efficient drainage system was maintained to let used water flow outside the city. Drinking water was supplied door to door through a pipeline connected to a water source in a mountain. Beautiful waterfalls were constructed at crossroads. At night ten thousand lamps were lit in the city and neighborhood at both sides of the roads. The Green Palace (*Qasr al-Zahra*) thrilled the visitors beyond imagination.[39]

Hakam al-Thani (961-976 A.D.), son of Abdur Raman lll, promoted and popularized education to the highest possible level.[40] The literacy rate among Muslims at that time was 100%. His personal interest in learning engendered great admiration for scholarship in the society. He greatly developed Cordova University founded by his father Abdur Rahman lll. Local students as well as those from other European countries thronged the university; best teachers from different countries were hired to teach there. He was so passionate about books that he deputed his men in different countries, like Egypt, Syria and Iraq, to buy books for him from there. There were six-hundred thousand titles in his personal library.

When the power in the center weakened, the provinces started separating from it by declaring themselves independent. But even in the days of this disintegration the new states maintained their patronage of literature and learning. The rulers of these states were themselves learned

---

[39] Siddiqui and Hasrat, p. 221.
[40] Siddiqui and Hasrat, p. 222.

people and tried to excel each other in patronizing literature and arts.[41]

When Grenada (*Gharnaata*) broke away from the center and became an independent state under Muhammad bin Yusuf (known also as Ibn al-Ahmar), he constructed there the famous Alhambra Palace, an architectural monument which is one of its kind in the world in beauty and grandeur and is a sign of Muslims' exquisite taste in architecture in which they have surpassed other civilizations.[42]

The Glories of Muslim Spain

Muslims introduced in Spain rice, sugarcane, saffron, peaches, pomegranate, pear, date, oranges and several other fruits and vegetables, which were unknown to the land. The government also encouraged people to adopt animal husbandry as profession: good breeds of animals, especially goat, sheep, and cow, were popularized.

Muslims also established industries in Spain, small and large. High quality Silken, woolen and cotton cloths were manufactured at a large scale there and exported to neighboring countries where they were in great demand. Silk worm was also reared at a large scale to obtain silk from them. Muslims learned making paper from China and established

---

[41] Siddiqui and Hasrat, p. 224.
[42] Siddiqui and Hasrat, p. 229.

paper factories in Spain, which significantly contributed to publishing of books and spreading of knowledge in society. They also established sugar, leather, glass, iron and marble factories.

Muslims took interest in mining as well. Elegant stones used in jewelry, magnetic stones, gold, silver, iron, copper, crystal glass, mercury and Sulphur were obtained from local mines. They were used in local factories as raw material; finished products prepared from them were mainly exported abroad. Muslims had a large fleet of commercial ships to facilitate their export and import activities. They earned a large profit by trade.

The lifestyle of people reflected prosperity, sophistication and refinement.[43] The houses were in general spacious, clean, and well-furnished. Generally, a house had a backyard garden. People commonly used carpet and ate with fork and knife. Educational and medical facilities were available free of cost. Starvation was rooted out from the society. Peace and security prevailed everywhere.

The society was fully inclusive, accommodating the Jews and the Christians without any bias and discrimination. Non-Muslim students studied at the universities of Spain with Muslims in a free and friendly environment. Women enjoyed a great amount of freedom. Education was quite popular among

---

[43] Siddiqui and Hasrat, pp. 232- 233.

women many of them distinguished themselves in poetry and other branches of learning.

Among the Spanish scholars Ibn Baja, Ibn Rushd, Ibn Zuhr, Zahrawi, and Ibn Baytar were distinguished in philosophy, medicine, surgery and other fields. Idrisi and Ibn Jubayr were famous names in the field of geography, and Ibn Khaldun was held as father of modern philosophy of history in Europe. The famous religious scholars Imam Ibn Hazm and Sheikh Mohiuddin Arabi lived in this very period. As poet, the name of Ibn Zaidun commanded highest respect.

....

The Muslim rule in Spain came to an end on 2 January 1492 A.D. which marks the termination of Muslim power in Europe. But around the same time Muslims established three empires in the East: The Ottoman Empire in Turkey, the Safavid Empire in Iran and the Mughal Empire in India. The Ottoman Empire was the religious guardian of Muslims all over the world, the Safavids established a powerful empire in Iran, and the Mughals built a huge empire in India, which included the present India, Pakistan, Bangla Desh and Afghanistan; they united separate independent states under one central rule and made it a nation that we call India. In all these countries great cultural renaissance, educational awakening and financial prosperity were witnessed. In this very period India was called "the golden bird" and saw the construction of the Red Fort of Delhi, the Qutub Minar of Fatahpur Sikri, the magnificent Fort of Agra, the Taj Mahal of Agra and many distinguished monuments. In the thirteenth and fourteenth centuries Islam also emerged as the choicest religion of the people in countries like Indonesia and Malaysia.

This point deserves special attention that the history of Islam is not merely the history of the Arabs. The Muslim states mentioned above, and those which emerged later, were, in fact, founded by people of different races and nationalities, such as the Turks, the Afghans, the Persians, the Berbers, and the slaves, including of course the Arabs. It was, in fact, only the religion of Islam that was common in them and inspired them to come up with such achievements.

True, the governments after the period of the Rightly-guided Caliphate did not remain *Islamic* one hundred percent, but they never officially broke away from Islam. They surely failed, and failed seriously, in fully adhering to the teachings of Islam in running the state, but Islam kept on guiding their course of action at moral, social and religious level and remained the main controlling force. The downfall of the Muslim empires was not the failure of Islam. Islam as religion kept on inspiring people and winning converts even in rough times.

Due to lack of space, we will not venture to discuss the periods after the Muslim rule in Spain. The above discussion of the Muslim rule from the days of the Prophet to the Muslim rule in Spain, which covers the length of a century, shows that the Muslim civilization was religiously tolerant, morally profound, socially inclusive and politically humane. The

Muslim states patronized progress and ensured prosperity for all citizens, Muslims as well as non-Muslims.

In the succeeding pages we will look at how Modern Western Civilization, which accuses Muslims of being "fundamentally incapable of joining global civilization," nay, lacking "the fundamental humanity",[44] is itself hugely indebted to Islamic Civilization. It would not have come into being, had Europe not come in contact with Muslims.

---

[44] For these accusations, see "Introduction" of this book.

(III)

ROLE OF MUSLIMS IN CREATING RENAISSANCE IN EUROPE

It is an interesting part of history that it was Muslims who initiated Renaissance in Europe by creating a scientific spirit of research and investigation in Europeans which helped them develop modern Western civilization, although it later assumed an extreme materialistic character on its own. When Muslim civilization flourished in Spain in the Middle Ages, people from different Europeans countries came there seeking education, as education was available to them only through the Muslims at that time. Dr. Tara Chand, a famous Indian historian, has acknowledged the debt that the West owes to Muslim scholars in the following words:

> For a thousand years this civilization [the Muslim civilization of Spain] was the central light whose rays illumined the world. It was the mother of European culture, for men reared in this civilization were the masters in the Middle Ages at whose feet the Spaniards,

the French, the English, the Italians and the Germans sat to learn philosophy, sciences of mathematics, astronomy, chemistry, physics, medicine and industrial techniques. Their names are household words.[45]

Western civilization identifies itself as a brainchild of Greco-Roman civilization, which it actually is. But the fact remains that the Greek knowledge did not reach Europeans directly through the Greeks; it reached them through the Muslims. When the Greek civilization saw its disintegration, the works of the Greek masters also suffered negligence and natural decay. The Roman Civilization, which succeeded Greek civilization, had no appreciation for learning and did not do anything to protect the academic legacy of the Greeks. The Muslims came into power after the Romans and it is their good work that they saved the Greek masterpieces by translating them into Arabic. Below we will show how important this contribution of Muslims proved for Europe.

1. PROTECTION OF GREEK LITERATURE IN THE FORM OF TRANSLATION

When the Muslims faced the Romans in the battlefield, they fought to subjugate the Romans, but they carefully collected

---

[45] Presidential Address, Fourth All India Islamic Studies Conference, 25-27 December, 1964, Osmania University, Hyderabad, p. 23, quoted by Ziauddin Ahmad, *Influence of Islam on World Civilization* (New Delhi, Adam Publishers and Distributers, 2006), p. xx.

the valuable writings of the Greeks they came across there and decided to save them from being lost. They brought them to their country and transferred them to Arabic. The Caliph Harun al-Rashid also personally requested the Roman emperor, with whom he had a peace treaty, to lend him books of Greek scholars for this purpose. He established an institution called *Darul Hikmah*, which Robert Briffault translates as "House of Science,"[46] in Baghdad in A.D. 833 where the works of Aristotle, Galen, Ptolemy and many other Greek writers were translated into Arabic. Philip Hitti writes that *Darul Hikmah* was a "combination of library, academy and translation bureau which in many respects proved the most important educational institution since the foundation of the Alexandrian Museum in the first half the third century B.C."[47]

> The translation work began in fact in the Abbasid era in 750 A.D. and continued for about one hundred years. For practical purposes, most of the translations were first done from Greek to Aramaic, the language of the time, which were thereafter translated into Arabic. Naturally Muslims had to seek the help of non-Muslim scholars who knew Greek, Aramaic and Arabic, which they did in the best academic spirit. They appointed Hunayn ibn-Ishaq (Joannitius), a Nestorian Christian, as the Chief of the Translators (*Sheikhul Mutarjimīn*); other

---

[46] Robert Briffault devotes a full section to *Darul-Hikmat* in his famous book *The Making of Humanity* from page 184 to 203.

[47] Hitti, pp. 117-18.

Christian and Jewish scholars were also taken in.[48] The Caliph Mamūn used to reward Hunayn by giving him gold equal to the weight of each book that he translated from Greek to Arabic. Mamūn also used to pay him a large salary.[49]

Hunayn translated the works of Galen, Hippocrates and Dioscorides, and also Plato's *Republic* and Aristotle's *Categories*, *Physics* and *Magna Moralia*. He also rendered into Arabic almost all of Galen's scientific writings, and the seven books of Galen's anatomy which survive now only in Arabic; the original works in Greek were long lost.[50] All these works reached Europe through Spain (which was under the Muslim rule at that time), where they were translated into European languages. These works stirred interest in science in Europe and paved the way for the creation of the Renaissance which, consequently, led to the creation of Modern Western Civilization. Briffault writes: "It is highly probable that but for the Arabs, modern European civilization would never have arisen at all; it is absolutely certain that but for them, it would not have assumed that character which has enabled it to transcend all previous phases of evolution."[51] Briffault also

------

[48] Hitti, pp. 117-18.

[49] Hitti, p. 91. It is a proof of Muslims' religious magnanimity that Mamun requested Hunayn to translate the Bible from Greek into Arabic. Hunayn complied. Unfortunately this translation is not extant now.

[50] Hitti, p. 119.

[51] Robert Briffault, *The Making of Humanity* (London: George Allen & Unwin, 1919), p. 90.

writes that Islam's influence on Europe is far greater than what is generally believed. He says: "It was not science which brought Europe back to life. Other and manifold influences from the civilization of Islam communicated its first glow to European life."[52]

2. ADDITIONS MADE BY MUSLIMS TO GREEK KNOWLEDGE

Some Western scholars have tried to belittle the contribution of Muslims in the advancement of Greek knowledge by arguing that Muslims were merely the transmitters of Greek knowledge to Europe by translating Greek masterpieces into Arabic. If Muslims had done only that, the West should acknowledge this debt with gratitude. Hitti acknowledges this fact in these words: "And transmission, from the standpoint of the history of culture, is no less essential than origination, for had the researches of Aristotle, Galen and Ptolemy been lost to posterity the world would have been as poor as if they had never been produced. The line of demarcation between translated and original work is, of course, not always clearly drawn. Many of the translators were also contributors.[53]

---

[52] Briffault, p. 202.
[53] Hitti, p. 141.

In fact, Muslim scholars made significant contributions by adding very informative commentaries and appendices to the Greek books they rendered into Arabic. As Hitti writes: "Their translations, modified by the Arab minds in the course of several centuries, were passed on, together with many new contributions, to Europe through Syria, Spain and Sicily and laid the basis of that canon of knowledge which dominated medieval European thought".[54]

It is a fact that if the appendices and commentaries added by Muslim translators to their translations of the Greek works were published separately, they would have been as valuable as independent original writings. But in those days, this was the way of writing and the value of addition of information in the form of appendices and commentaries was appreciated as original contribution.

3. ORIGINAL RESEARCH AND PUBLICATIONS OF MUSLIM SCHOLARS

In addition to translations, Muslims also conducted original researches and wrote pioneering books in Arabic in various fields which were later translated in European languages.

---

[54] Hitti, p. 141.

Unfortunately, it has been a general trend in Europe to ignore the value and originality of the Arabic works produced by the Muslims. Montgomery Watt comments on it in these words: "[T]here still remains a certain tendency to belittle the work of the Arabs (in the sense of Muslim writing in Arabic), and to regard them as no more than transmitters of Greek ideas." Watt mentions Carra de Voux, a famous scholar on Muslim contributions in science, who in his famous article "Astronomy and Mathematics," included in *The Lagacy of Islam*, downgrades the Arab scholars as mere transmitters, humble disciples of the Greeks whose contributions cannot be considered original. But, as Watt puts it, "a moment later, however, he [Carra de Voux] concedes that 'the Arabs have really achieved great things in science'". Watt recounts that in medicine alone, "from 800 to 1300 medical writings in Arabic have been preserved from the pens of over seventy authors, mostly Muslims, but including a few Christians and Jews."[55]

Tracing the influence of the Arabs on Europe in historical perspective, Briffault writes: "Arabian knowledge began at an early date to percolate into Christian Europe. If there be any ground of fact in the legend of alchemical pursuits of St. Dunstan, Arabian lore must have been much more widely diffused in the tenth century than can be shown by surviving records."[56]

---

[55] W. Montgomery Watt, *The Majesty That Was Islam* (London: Sidgwick & Jackson, 1984), pp. 226-27.

[56] Briffault, p. 198.

Hitti also acknowledges the original contributions of Muslims in Arabic which influenced the world of learning at a very large scale. He says: "For several centuries it [Arabic] was the language of learning, culture and progressive thought throughout the civilized world. Between the ninth and the twelfth centuries more works – philosophical, medical, historical, religious, astronomical and geographical – were produced through the medium of Arabic than through any other tongue. The vocabularies of European languages bear the marks of its influence."[57]

The Arabic books served as textbooks and references in European universities for centuries. Briffault writes that up until the fifteenth century the research work was based on the Arabic books that the Muslim scholars had produced; nothing new of any significance came up.[58] Briffault takes up this issue in detail in *The Making of Humanity* (pp. 184-202) and mentions the books that Muslim scholars produced.

> In fact, the writings of the Arabs influenced young generations of Europeans deeply and extensively. Alvaro, a ninth century Cordovan bishop writes: "All the young Christians who distinguished themselves by their talent, know the language and literature of the Arabs, read and study passionately the Arab books, gather at

---

[57] Hitti, p. 6. Muslims also rendered into Arabic some important works from the Pahlavi and Sanskrit languages. But as we are concerned with Islam's influence on Europe in this book, we do not deal with them here.

[58] Briffault, p. 202.

great expense great libraries of these, and everywhere proclaim with a loud voice how admirable is that literature."[59]

Briffault mentions the beneficiaries from the Western world, Gerbert of Aurillac (Pope Sylvester II), Constantine, an African monk, Adelhard of Bath and several others, who popularized Arabic books in Europe. He, for example, writes about Constantine: "An African monk, Constantine, who had acted as secretary to Robert Guiscard, devoted himself with enthusiasm to the translation of Arab textbooks and to introducing the new learning into the mother house of the Benedictines at Monte Casino, whence the path lay open for its transmission to the far-flung houses of the order." About Adelhard of Bath he writes that he "brought with him from Cordova a large collection of books and much doctrine, which he and his nephew actively spread abroad in France and England."[60]

We will also discuss some important books written by Muslim scholars in Part IV.

Muslims also established great universities in which Europeans acquired knowledge and training that prepared them to start a scientific revolution in Europe. Briffault writes: "From all parts of Europe numerous students betook

---

[59] Briffault, p. 198.
[60] Briffault, pp. 189-90.

themselves to the great Arab seats of learning in search of the light which only there was to be found."[61]

4. INTRODUCTION OF EXPERIMENTAL METHOD

The greatest contribution of Muslims in the field of science, however, was introduction of Experimental Method in the field of research by which they created what is now called science. The work of the Greeks was theoretical. Muslims formulated hypotheses on the basis of their theories and tested them through experiments to determine their validity. The works of the Greeks were never works of science; in fact, the Greek period was pre-scientific.[62] Briffault writes: "Not only did the Arabs create those mathematics which were to be the indispensable instrument of scientific analysis, they laid the foundation of those methods of experimental research which in conjunction with mathematical analysis gave birth to modern science."[63]

Briffault elaborates this point in the following passage: "They [the Arabs] accepted the conclusions of the Greeks as

---

[61] Briffault, p. 198.
[62] Briffault, p. 191.
[63] Briffault, p. 194.

working theories necessary to the pursuit of scientific enquiry, only venturing to criticize or modify them as the expansion of knowledge forced them to adapt them to new facts."[64] The Greeks and the Romans did not come up with any invention. Inventions began with Muslims. It was Muslims who invented gun-powder, mariner's compass, surgery apparatuses and many other important things which gave a boost to discoveries, researches and spread of knowledge.[65]

It will not be out of place to mention here that some Western writers push forth the name of Roger Bacon as the founder of Experimental Method in order to discredit the Muslims. However, this has been regretted by informed and objective Western scholars as well. Briffault comments on it in these words:

> Neither Roger Bacon nor his later namesake has any title to be credited with having introduced the experimental method.... Discussions as to who was the originator of the experimental method, like the fostering of every Arab discovery or invention on the first European who happens to mention it, such as the invention of the compass to a fabulous Flavio Gioja of Amalfi, of alcohol to Arnold of Villeneuve, of lenses and gunpowder to Bacon or Schwartz, are part of the colossal misrepresentation of the origins of European civilization.

---

[64] Briffault, p. 192.
[65] Briffault, pp. 206-07.

The experimental method of Arabs was by Bacon's time widespread and eagerly cultivated throughout Europe.[66]

---

[66] Briffault, pp. 200-201.

(IV)

MUSLIM CONTRIBUTION TO SCIENCE

Muslims have a very strong claim to be the pioneers in the field of science. Briffault acknowledges it in most explicit words. He says: "The debt of our science to that of the Arabs does not consist in startling discoveries or revolutionary theories; science owes a great deal more to Arab culture, it owes its existence. The ancient world was, as we saw, pre-scientific."[67]

1. CREATION OF SCIENCE

Briffault emphasizes the importance of Experimental Method in the creation of science and argues that it was the Muslims who introduced it first as a necessary step to verify the validity of a theory. He says: "What we call science arose in Europe as a result of a new spirit of inquiry, of new methods of investigation, of the methods of experiment, observation,

---

[67] Briffault, p. 191.

measurement, of the development of mathematics in a form unknown to the Greeks. That spirit and those methods were introduced into the European world by the Arabs."[68]

Briffault also says that the credit for the birth of the Renaissance in Europe, which ushered scientific pursuit there, goes to the Muslim Spain, not to Italy. He writes: "It was under the influence of the Arabs and the Moorish revival of culture and not in the 15th century, that a real Renaissance took place. Spain, not Italy, was the cradle of the rebirth of Europe."[69]

The theories developed in Greece did not become popular during the Roman regime. Max Meyerhof writes, "By the time the Arabs had penetrated into the Byzantine and Persian Empires, Greek science had for centuries ceased to be a living force."[70] The Romans were not very much interested in learning. Also, after the Roman emperor Constantine accepted Christianity, which then became the state religion, science was denied its basic right of survival. The Church punished the supporters of science as heretics, which forced people having scientific inclination to leave the country. Egypt, which was under the Roman Empire in those days, was a typical case in point. In the words of Meyerhof, "Egypt, however, provided on the one hand a population fanatically Christian, and on the

---

[68] Briffault, p. 191.

[69] Briffault, p. 188.

[70] Max Meyerhof, "Science and Medicine," in *Legacy of Islam* (henceforth referred as *Legacy*), by Arnold Sir Alfred Thomas and Guillaume (New Delhi, Kitab Bhavan, 2009), p. 312.

other abounded in occultism and mysticism. The soil was not favorable for any scientific development."[71]

It was Muslims who by using Experimental Method revolutionized the world and established the credibility of science. They tested Greek theories, approved of them if they were correct, and corrected them if they had an error. They, for example, "accepted Ptolemy's cosmology, but not his catalogue of stars or his planetary table, or his measurements. They drew up new star catalogues, correcting and greatly amplifying; they compiled new sets of planetary tables.... They devised for the carrying out of those observations elaborate instruments superior to those of the Greeks and exceeding in accuracy those manufactured in the fifteenth century at the famous Nuremberg factory."[72] That is why Gustav Le Bon calls Muslims "Europe's Professor."[73]

2. MUSLIM SCIENTISTS AND RESEARCHERS

The galaxy of Muslim scientists and researchers is large and luminous, but due to the limitation of space we will discuss below only a few selected ones. Needless to say that these writers produced their researches in Arabic.

---

[71] Meyerhof, p. 312.

[72] Briffault, pp. 192-93.

[73] Gustav le Bon, quoted by Sayyed Mujtaba Musavi in *Western Civilization Through Muslim Eyes*, transl. by F. J Gouling (Qom, Foundation of Islamic C. P. W., 2008), pp. 74-75.

Razi (Rhazes: 865-925AD)

Razi, or Rhazes as he is called in the West, was, in the words of Max Meyerhof, "undoubtedly the greatest physician of the Islamic world and one of the great physicians of all time."[74] He is credited for having produced more than two hundred books, half of which were on medicine.

He wrote a very valuable book on measles and small pox in Arabic called *Aljudri wal Husba*, which was translated into English as *On Small-pox and Measles*. In it he dismissed the traditional myth that these diseases were brought upon the patient by an angry god and argued that they were, in fact, contagious diseases which could be treated by medicine. This book was translated into Latin, from which it was rendered into several European languages, including English. Between 1498 A.D. and 1866 A.D. it was published in translation forty times in Europe.[75] This book led to the discovery of the treatment of these diseases.

Rhazes also wrote a book on pediatrics which was acknowledged as the first book on this topic. He was the first person to use injection for treating certain diseases. He was also interested in surgery and had invented seton, a needle to open wounds. He had penned down many other books which did not survive the ravages of time.

---

[74] Meyerhof, p. 323.
[75] Meyerhof, p. 323.

Rhazes also wrote books on chemistry which made a breakthrough in the field. His book *Kitabul Asraar*, translated into English as *The Book of Secrets,* is very famous. Gerard of Cremona rendered it into Latin in the twelfth century. It remained an important reference book for Europeans up until the fourteenth century. The famous Western writer Roger Bacon quotes it in *De spirtibus et corporibus.*[76]

But Rhazes' greatest contribution was *Al-Hawi* (*Comprehensive Book*). It was in twenty volumes out of which only ten are extant. It was first rendered into Latin in 1279 A.D. by Farragut (Farj bin Salim), a Jewish scholar of Sicily. After 1486 A.D. several editions of this book appeared under the title *Continens*. In 1542 A.D. it was published for the fifth time from Venice in Paris. It was an encyclopedic work and contained exhaustive information on medicine available by that time from Greek, Persian and Indian sources. Rhazes added his own observations and researches at the end of the book and also gave suggestions for the treatment of diseases. This work remained a very valuable source of information for Europeans for centuries.[77]

Ibn Sina (Avicenna: 980-1037 AD)

Abu Ali al-Husayn ibn Sina, called Avicenna in the West, may be called the second most respected Muslim scholar in

---

[76] Hitti, p. 143.
[77] Meyerhof, pp. 324-25.

medicine. He was a philosopher, astronomer, mathematician and poet, but was at his best in medicine. Two of his books on medicine were very influential: *Al-Shifa* (*Book of Healing*) and *Al-Qanun fit Tib* (*The Canon of Medicine*). *The Canon* won him higher acclaim in the West. An encyclopedic work in scope, it covered description of the diseases relating to each organ of the human body. In the last thirty years of the fifteenth century a Hebrew and fifteen Latin editions of this book were published in Europe. A partial translation of this book in English appeared in 1930 A.D. which carried the title *A Treatise on the Canons of Medicine of Avicenna*. Dr. Robinson says that "the *Canon of Avicenna*, consisting of approximately a million words, is the most influential textbook ever written; for six centuries it dominated the medical schools of Asia and Europe."[78] As Dr. William Oslar, author of *The Evolution of Modern Science*, puts it, "*the Qanun* has remained a medical Bible for longer period than any other work."[79]

Ibn Sina was the first to invent a catheter (a thin tube put into the body to remove liquid, such as urine) from animal skin and mentioned intravesical injections. Further details of his contributions can be seen in Ziauddin Ahmad.[80]

Mentioning the popularity of Razi and Ibn Sina, Philip Hitti writes: "The portraits of two of these, Rhazes and

---

[78] Ziauddin Ahmad, *Influence of Islam on World Civilization* (New Delhi, Adam Publishers and Distributers, 2006), p. 133.
[79] Ahmad, p. 134.
[80] Ahmad, pp. 132-33.

Avicenna, adorn the great hall of the School of Medicine at the University of Paris."[81]

Ibn Khatima (d. 1369 AD)

Ibn Khatima of Muslim Spain was another medical researcher who further investigated the causes and treatment of plague and studied the plague that had spread in Almeria in Spain during 1348 and 1349 A.D. Ibn Khatima confirmed that it was a contagious disease and could be treated. Max Meyerhof writes that Ibn Khatima's book on small pox was the best among all the books written on this subject between fourteenth century and sixteenth century. Meyerhof also presents an extract of this book in his well-known essay "Science and Medicine" which is included in the anthology *The Legacy of Islam.* He mentions that the Greek masters of medicine had simply not paid attention to the contagious nature of plague and scholars of the medieval period also passed over it without investigating this aspect of it.[82]

Jabir bin Hayyan (Geber: 8th century)

Jabir (Geber) is a very prominent figure in the history of chemistry. Chemistry before him was drenched in superstitious traditions. It was Jabir who transformed it into a

---

[81] Hitti, p. 142.
[82] Meyerhof, pp. 340-41.

scientific study of metals and matter. His chief contribution was the introduction of Experimental Method for investigating a theoretical assumption, due to which he was acknowledged as "the father of Arabic alchemy" in Europe.[83] The fact that this branch of science is still called "alchemy," a derivative of the Arabic word "alkemiya," and the presence of a large number of Arabic terms in modern chemistry testifies to the Arab influence on its evolution and progress.

Jabir's books on chemistry were translated into Latin through which the West came to learn about his researches and investigations. His book, *Book of Composition and Alchemy*, was translated by Robert of Chestor, the first edition of which appeared in 1144 A.D. Jabir's another book, *Book of the Seventy*, was rendered into Latin by Gerard of Cremona. Yet another book of Jabir, *The Sum of Perfection*, was translated by Richard Russell in 1678. Ziauddin Ahmad provides interesting details about Jabir's works in his book *Influence of Islam on World Civilization,* pp. 186-87. One of Jabir's books, *Book of the Art*, has been recently discovered.[84]

Al-Khwarizmi (780-850 AD)

Alkhwarizmi (Abu Jafar Abdullah Muhammad bin Musa) is mentioned by Philip Hitti as "one of the greatest minds of Islam." His contributions to the development of mathematics

---

[83] Meyerhof, p. 327.
[84] Ahmad, p. 187.

in Europe were monumental and had profound and far-reaching effects on the promotion of learning. Hitti writes:

> Apart from compiling the oldest astronomical tables, al-Khwarizmi composed the oldest work on arithmetic and the oldest work on algebra, which was translated into Latin and used until the sixteenth century as the principal mathematical textbook of European universities and served to introduce into Europe the science of algebra, and with it the name. His works were also responsible for the introduction into the West of the Arabic numerals, called "algorisms" after him. Zero or cipher (Arabic *sifr*) was also then introduced.[85]

Khwarizmi wrote a book on algebra entitled *Al-Jabr wal Maqalaat* in which he presented algebraic concepts in a very lucid and organized way. Carra de Vaux speaks highly of the depth and soundness of al-Khwarizmi's work.[86]

Al-Khwarizmi is also considered founder of the science of trigonometry. The sine and trigonometry tables were his very valuable contributions. His trigonometrical tables were translated by Adelard of Bath which greatly benefited the West.[87]

---

[85] Hitti, pp. 146-47.

[86] Carra de Voux, "Astronomy and Mathematics," in *Legacy of Islam,* by Alfred Arnold Sir Thomas and Guillaume (New Delhi, Kitab Bhavan, 2009), pp. 381-86.

[87] Md. R. Mirza and Mohd. Iqbal Siddiqui, *Muslim Contribution to Science*, (New Delhi, Adam Publishers, 2005), pp. 6-7.

Khwarizmi also made valuable contributions in the field of geography. When the Caliph Mamun started a project for measuring the circumference of the earth, Khwarizmi was also a member of the team. Al-Khwarizmi also wrote a book *Mafatihul Uloom* (*Keys of the Sciences*). His writings opened the door for further research.

Ibn Al-Haytham (Alhazen: 968-1039)

Abu Ali al-Hasan Ibn Al-Haytham (Alhazen) was from Basra and lived in Egypt in the Fatimid period. His contribution in the field of optics was monumental. He differed from the theory of Euclid and Ptolemy, famous Greek masters, that light was discharged from the eye and encircled the object in order to recognize it. He argued that as a matter of fact the form of the object came to the eye which it analyzed by means of its relevant apparatuses in order to recognize it. One of his views is still known as "Al-Hazen's Problem" in the West. Max Meyerhof says that Al-Hazen had reached quite close to the discovery of magnifying lenses, but he died before bringing his research to completion. After his death the discovery of magnifying lenses was delayed for centuries. It was well after three centuries that work on it was resumed in Italy which was completed after six centuries when Snell and Descartes formulated law of sines.[88]

---

[88] Meyerhof, p. 334.

Al-Haytham wrote forty-four books on philosophy, geometry, astronomy and mechanics.[89] But he was especially credited for having written *Optics* which opened the door for new researches in the field. Meyerhof writes: "Roger Bacon (thirteenth century) and all medieval writers on optics – notably the Pole Witelo or Vitellio – base their optical works largely on Alhazen's *Opticae Thesaurus*. His work also influenced Leonardo da Vinci and Johann Keplar."[90]

Al-Haytham's short books on physical optics reflected his sharp scientific investigative mind. In one of these, *On Twilight Phenomena*, now extant only in Latin, he stated that the height of the atmosphere was ten English miles. He had constructed mirrors of metal to study the reflection of light. In *On the Burning Glass* he "created a dioptric far superior to that of the Greeks." He researched the image of the sun during eclipse by taking its image on a wall which Meyerhof calls "the first record of the *camera obscura*."[91]

Abdul Latif al-Baghdadi (1162- 1231 AD)

Al-Baghdadi is a famous name in anatomy. He traveled from Baghdad to Egypt to benefit from the scholars there and wrote an account of his travel (and about the famine that had befallen Egypt in those days). In Egypt he spent a good deal of

---

[89] Ahmad, p. 137.
[90] Meyerhof, p. 334.
[91] Meyerhof, p. 335.

time in studying the remains of the human body in a graveyard, on the basis of which he, in the words of Meyerhof, "checked and corrected Galen's description of the bone of the lower jaw and of the sacrum."[92] Ziauddin Ahmad also refers to this event: "Abdul Latif made a scientific study of human skeletons accidentally discovered in a large pit at Al-Max (Egypt) and made note of much important facts." He writes that this event led to the birth of the discipline of postmortem, which was adopted in Europe much later.[93]

Ibn Al-Baytar (d. 1248 AD)

Ibn Al-Baytar is a prestigious name in botany. He traveled to different countries in order to discover the medical properties of plants and drugs and performed first-hand tests on them. In his famous book *A Collection of Simple Drugs* he mentioned the result of his research on 1400 plants and drugs which he personally investigated in his journey between Spain and Syria. Meyerhof writes: "It is a work of extraordinary erudition and observation, and is the greatest of the Arabic books on botany."[94] Syed Ameer Ali also speaks of the interest that Muslim scholars took in investigating the medicinal value of plants and drugs. He says: "Botany they advanced far beyond the state in which it had been left by Dioscorides, and

---

92 Meyerhof, p. 336.
93 Ahmad, p. 145.
94 Meyerhof, p. 339.

augmented the herbology of the Greeks by the addition of two thousand plants. Regular gardens existed both in Cordova and Baghdad, at Cairo and Fez for the education of pupils, where discourses were delivered by the most learned in the sciences."[95]

Al-Beruni (973-1048 AD)

Abu Rayhan Muhammad Al-Beruni, who was attached to the court of Sultan Mahmood Ghaznawi, wrote about one hundred and eighty books on different topics. He was a physician, astronomer, mathematician, physicist, geographer and historian and was called "the Master" (*al-Ustad*).[96] He is also credited for having written a travelogue, *Tarikh al-Hind*, which contained very valuable information about India and was translated in English by Dr. Edward Sachau. An English translation of one of his books, *Kitab al-Tafhim li Awaili Sina'at al-Tanjim*, was published by Ramsay Wright, London, in 1939 A.D. He also wrote a comprehensive book on astronomy called *Al-Qanun al-Mas'udi fi al-Hayaat wan Najm*. Two of his writings, *Chronology of Ancient Nations* and *History of India* are available to the modern world in good translation. Recently, in 1948, a volume containing four of his books was

---

[95] Syed Ameer Ali, *The Spirit of Islam* (Calcutta, S. K. Lahiri & Co., 1902), p. 357.

[96] Ahmad, p. 103.

published from Hyderabad.[97] His book on mathematics has not yet been published.

His great contribution in physics lay in the fact that he determined the correct weight of eighteen precious stones and metals. An unedited lapidary by him, containing information about a large number of stones and metals, is in Escorial Library.[98]

Al-Mas'udi (957 AD)

Abul Hasan Ali Ibn al-Husain al-Mas'udi was born in Baghdad and died in Egypt and was a reputed scientist of his time. He wrote two great books. His first book, *Meadows of Gold*, was in thirty volumes, an English translation of which was published by Sprenger from London in 1842. Max Meyerhof writes, "In his *Meadows of Gold* he [Al-Mas'udi] described an earthquake, the waters of the Dead Sea, and the first windmills, which are perhaps an invention of Islamic peoples, and he also gives what has been described as the rudiments of a theory of evolution."[99] His second book *Kitab al-Tanbih* was a masterpiece which was translated into French by the famous French scholar Carra de Voux at Paris in 1896. De Goeji brought it out editing it as Volume VIII of the *Bibliotheca Geographorum Arabicorum*.[100]

---

[97] Ahmad, p. 103
[98] Meyerhof, p. 332.
[99] Meyerhof, p. 333.

Abu al-Qasim al-Zahrawi (Abulcasis: 939-1013)

Abu al Qasim al-Zahrawi is considered as the greatest surgeon of the Islamic history. He was from Cordova in Spain and was attached to the court of the Caliph Al-Hakam. He produced an encyclopedic work, *Kitab al-Tasrif* (*Medical Vade Mecum*), which was in thirty volumes. The thirtieth volume, "fil 'amal bil yadd," was translated in French at Paris in 1861. Western scholars greatly benefited from this book. The part specifically dealing with surgery in *Al-Tasrif* was rendered into Latin from Arabic by Gerard of Cremona, which was published from different places in Europe from the fifteenth century to the eighteenth and was used as textbook at educational institutions. The pictures of about two hundred surgical apparatuses are included in this book.

Abu al-Qasim greatly influenced the study of medicine in Europe. As Meyerhof writes about him, "his work contained illustrations of instruments which influenced other Arabic authors and especially helped to lay the foundation of surgery in Europe. It was translated into Latin, Provencal and Hebrew. The celebrated French surgeon Guy de Chauliac (1300-68) appended the Latin version to one of his works."[101] Ziauddin Ahmad introduces Guy de Chauliac as "the father of French surgery" and states that he mentioned Abu al-Qasim more than 200 times in his works.[102]

---

[100] Ahmad, p. 201.
[101] Meyerhof, p. 331.

Omar Khayyam (d. 1123)

Carra de Voux writes that Omar Khayyam's book on geometry showed his depth of knowledge, soundness of argument and sharpness of perception. Similarly, his book on algebra was a work in which he surpassed Greek scholars, even Khwarizmi. Omar Khayyam's book on algebra was translated and edited in French by F. Woepcke, which was published from Paris in 1857. Meyerhof has given some examples of Omar Khayyam's superiority to the Greeks in the treatment of algebra in his essay "Astronomy and Mathematics," which is included in *Legacy of Islam*. Khayyam also prepared a calendar some six hundred years before the Gregorian calendar, which was superior to Gregorian calendar in many ways.[103]

Ibn -Rushd (Averroes: 1126-98 AD)

Ibn -Rushd is a very prestigious name in philosophy and is more popular in the West than in the East. He also took interest in medicine. He was the first to discover that small pox attacked a person only once in life. He also very accurately described the function of retina in the eye. But the West knew and recognized him best as the commentator on Aristotle: it was he who introduced the philosophy of Aristotle in Europe

---

102 Ahmad, p. 142. For more details about Abu al-Qasim's contributions, see Ziauddin Ahmad, pp. 139-42.

103 Ahmad, p. 104.

as his interpreter and it was his interpretation of Aristotelian philosophy which gained acceptance in Europe. Hitti writes: "From the end of the twelfth to the end of the sixteenth century Averroism remained the dominant school of thought [in Europe]." He writes further that "his writings became prescribed studies in the University of Paris and other institutions of higher learning…. [T]he intellectual movement initiated by Averroes continued to be a living factor in European thought until the birth of modern experimental science."[104]

Ibn Khaldun (1332-1406 AD)

Ibn Khaldun, born in Tunis in 1332 AD, was a graduate from Al-Azhar University of Cairo and was a *Hafiz* (one who commits to memory the whole Quran). He achieved fame and recognition mainly due to his *Muqaddamah* (*Prolegomena*) in which he presented a new theory of history writing. Hitti writes, "No Arab writer, indeed no European, had ever before taken a view of history at once so comprehensive and philosophic. By the consensus of all critical opinion, Ibn Khaldun, who died in 1406, was the greatest historical philosopher Islam produced and one of the greatest of all time."[105] M. Basharat 'Ali calls Ibn Khaldun "the first scientific historian and scientific sociologist of the modern world."[106]

---

104 Hitti, pp. 188-89.
105 Hitti, p. 181.

The above discussion shows the role the Muslims have played in the advancement of science. But we must not miss the point that their contribution was not limited merely to this field. As Briffault writes, "for although there is not a single aspect of European growth in which the decisive influence of Islamic culture is not traceable, nowhere is it so clear and momentous as in the genesis of that power which constitutes the paramount distinctive force of the modern world and the supreme source of its victory – natural science and the scientific spirit."[107]

---

[106] M. Basharat Ali, "Contribution of Muslims in the Field of Sociology," in *Muslim Contribution to Science*, by Md. R. Mirza, and Siddiqui and Mohd. Iqbal (New Delhi, Adam Publishers, 2005), p. 251.
[107] Briffault, p. 190.

(V)

CONCLUSION

1. FUTURE OF ISLAM: HOPES AND WORRIES

We argued above that Islam is a vibrant religion, capable of leadership in progress and securing comprehensive prosperity and happiness for all. But this is also a fact that Muslims now lag behind in progress at all fronts. The cause of their backwardness must be investigated, but that is not the issue we have taken up in this book. In it we are refuting the allegation that Muslims as a religious community are inherently incapable of espousing the ideology of progress. In order to show the absurdity of this allegation, we discussed above the progressive history of Muslims and their monumental contributions in important fields.

But a question confronts us at this point without handling which we cannot establish that Islam is an inherently progressive religion. We must find out if there is any hope for Muslims to regain their lost status in future, for if Islam is a viable and relevant religion, it should be able to help its followers out of this depressing situation. As the accusation of Muslims' irrelevance comes mainly from the West, we will check below what objective Western thinkers in general say about this issue.

Marcus Noland comments on this issue in these words: "Islam does not appear to be a drag on growth or an anchor of development as alleged. If anything, the opposite appears to be true."[108]

Commenting on the prospect of Islam's revival in future, the Catholic writer and Liberal MP, Hilaire Belloc (1870-1953), writes in his 1936 book entitled *The Great Heresies*:

> May not Islam arise again? In a sense the question is already answered because Islam has never departed. It still demands the fixed loyalty and unquestioning adhesion of all the millions between the Atlantic and the Indus and further afield throughout scattered communities of further Asia…. [F]or my part I cannot but believe that a main unexpected thing of the future is the return of Islam. Since religion is at the root of all political movements and changes and since we have here a very great religion physically paralyzed but morally intensely alive, we are in the presence of an unstable equilibrium which cannot remain permanently unstable….[109]

---

[108] Marcus Noland, "Religion, Culture and Economic Performance," Peterson Institute for International Economics, Washington, 2003, quoted by Ali A. Allawi, *The crisis of Islamic Civilization* (London, Yale University Press, 2009), p. 288, footnote 5.

Belloc is of opinion that Islam will surely stage a comeback, but there is a note of uneasiness in his prophesy as he sees Islam's revival as a prospective challenge to Christianity. Other Western writers have taken an unstintingly positive stand at this issue and suggested fairly strongly that Islam can reassert its identity on the world scene by virtue of its moral strength and spiritual excellence. Tin Wallace Murphy comments on this issue in these words:

> Can the world of Islam solve its own problems? It has done so in the past and, thanks to the basic principles of its faith, it has done so with tolerance and respect for other faiths and cultures, a lesson that the West has still to fully appreciate. Sustained by their firm and unshakable faith, and imbued with the desire for freedom, who or what can stop them? The religion of Islam has inspired so much in the past and it will triumph again in the fields where it has more experience than others – tolerance, creativity and respect. Grant them the same respect that they have shown to us when they, unconditionally, shared the fruits of their culture with us."[110]

---

[109] Ali A. Allawi, *The Crisis of Islamic Civilization*, (London, Yale University Press, 2009), p. 278, footnote No. 31.

[110] Tin Wallace Murphy, *What Islam Did for us* (London: Watkins Publishing, 2008), p. 217.

2. WORRIES CONCERNING EMERGENCE OF ISLAM

Some Western thinkers are of opinion that as Islam is not ready to modernize, Muslims deprive themselves of benefiting from the experiences of the West and lose the opportunity of coming out of their primitiveness and backwardness. Professor William E. Hocking of Harvard University, however, thinks differently and expresses his views on this issue in these words:

> Islamic lands will not progress by merely imitating Western arrangements and values. Can Islam produce fresh thinking, independent laws and relevant statutes to fit the new needs raised by modern society? Yes! – and more! Islam offers humanity greater possibilities for advance than others can. Its lack is not ability – but the will to use it. In reality, the Shar'iya contains all the ingredients needed.[111]

Significantly, Hawking mentions in the above quotation the Islamic Shariah and states that it surely has the potentiality to redress the woes of the modern world. This has been acknowledged by other Western scholars as well. In 1932 A.D. a world conference was held in the Hague to study Islamic *Fiqh*

---

[111] William E. Hawking, *The Spirit of World Politics*, quoted by Sayyed Mujtaba Musavi, in *Western Civilization Through Muslim Eyes*, transl. by F. J Gouling (Qom, Foundation of Islamic C. P. W, 2008), p. 62.

(Islamic Jurisprudence which is a part of Islamic Shariah), and in 1948 in the Hague again a world conference was called by the law experts for the same purpose in which representatives of fifty-three countries participated. On both occasions the participants acknowledged that Islamic *Fiqh* was truly relevant to the modern times and could sort out problems faced by the modern world.[112] Again, in 1951 the College of Law of Paris University in France invited experts from the whole world to review the relevance and potentiality of Islamic *Fiqh*. This conference was held for a whole week which was chaired by the Head of the Parisian Lawyers' Society. At the end of the conference the Chairman presented the following as a part of the final report:

> Let me sum up the new insights – new I think to most of us – the conference has given us, in this week devoted particularly to the Feqh, Islamic Canon Law. We saw in it a depth of rock bottom principle and of particularized care which embraces mankind in its universality and is thus able to give an answer to all the emergencies and events of this age. In our final communique we say: Islamic Canon Law should be made one of the formative elements of all new international legislation to meet present-day conditions, since it possesses a legal treasure of stable universal value which fits its Feqh,

---

[112] Sharqawi, Mohammad Ali, *Aalami Tahzibo Thiqafat par Islam ke athraat* (Urdu), transl. Suhayb Alam and Najmus Sehar (New Delhi: Al-Balaagh Publications, 2007), pp. 108-09.

amongst the modern welter of religious views and pronouncements, to cope with the exigencies imposed by the new forms of living arising in the modern environment.[113]

Some thinkers apprehend that if Islam regains power, it will clash with the present civilization and destroy its fabric of tolerance, inclusiveness and secularism. This apprehension, falsely generated by persistent anti-Islam campaign, has become a part of modern man's psyche, but history defies this untruth. Murphy says that "history has proved beyond all doubt that the world of Islam is founded on spiritual principles that have an innate capacity for fostering tolerance, understanding and promoting brotherhood between all races and creeds."[114]

When the Caliph Omar, and after him Salahuddin Ayyubi, conquered Jerusalem, they gave the Christians and the Jews the same right to visit the city and perform religious rituals there that the Muslims had.[115] Also, as Briffault writes, in the Muslim society of Spain the Christians lived in full harmony with Muslims: "Under absolute religious tolerance,

---

[113] Lari, p. 69.

[114] Murphy, p. 217.

[115] In order to appreciate Muslims' religious magnanimity, we may recall that when the Christians ruled Jerusalem, the Jews were not allowed to worship there in accordance with their religious teachings, and now when Jerusalem is under the control of the Jews, Muslims are not allowed to perform their religious rites there.

Christians enjoyed complete freedom in the Spanish Khalifate; they had their own bishop; several monasteries existed in the outskirts of the capital which served as hostels for travelers, and monks were commonly seen in the streets of Cordova." He writes further about the Jews: "The Jews shared under the complete tolerance of Moorish rule in the cultural evolution of the Khalifate."[116] Ernest Renan also acknowledges the religious magnanimity of Muslims. He writes about the ideal inclusiveness that prevailed in Muslim Spain by citing the example of Cordova: "Christians, Jews and Mussalmans [*sic*] spoke the same tongue, sang the same songs, [and] participated in the same literary and scientific studies. All the barriers which separated the various peoples were effaced; all worked with one accord in the work of a common civilization."[117]

The critics also question that if Islam is really so vibrant and the Islamic Canon Law, i. e., the *Shariah*, so progressive, why the Muslim states are in general sickly and backward. Ali A. Allawi looks at this question and comes to the conclusion that the political interference of Western powers in the affairs of Muslim states, negative and ill-intentioned, has played a strong role in creating this situation. He comments: "These tender shoots of an indigenous and authentic Islamic response to the political challenges of the modern era were snuffed out, partly through the reassertion of autocratic rule, but mostly

---

[116] Briffault, pp. 198-99.
[117] Ernest Renan, *Averroes et Averroism*, quoted by Ameer Ali, p.349.

through the destruction of the Islamic political space in the period after the First World War." The West imposed upon Muslim countries its ideologies, systems and institutions which "were all cast in the new political language drawn from the West, and were enacted in an environment which had been molded on the colonial and post-colonial experience." The result was the sad demise of the Muslim efforts: "Under such circumstances, the evolution of institutions which might have been both modern and within the spirit of Islamic legacy was impossible." Allawi concludes in these words: "From this perspective, the criticisms levelled at Islam's ability to generate political structures and doctrines consistent with the present global world view are seriously deficient."[118]

If Europe, let us assume, would have fallen under the dominance of an unfriendly political power in the mid-eighteenth century, "no one would have expected it to have produced the entire gamut of liberal democratic institutions and practice in the short term."[119] It is one thing to say that Islam has not developed a full-fledged philosophical, social and political structure similar to the Western one; it is an entirely different thing to assume that it cannot do so. Islam is the only religion that offers a full-fledged structure upon which a comprehensive civilization can be built.

---

[118] Allawi, p. 168.
[119] Allawi, p. 168.

Muslim states may rightly be criticized for autocracy that exists there in one form or another. But should Islam and its teachings be held responsible for this situation? Allawi says: "The typecasting of Islamic rule as entirely autocratic may be partly validated by history, but it is certainly not sanctioned either by the Quran or by the Prophet's sayings."[120] However, this is a fact that the autocratic rulers of the Muslim states are all existing at the life support provided by the West. The shahs and the sheikhs ruling Islamic lands are good friends of the Western champions of democracy.

3. WESTERN CIVILIZATION: AN APPRAISAL

The complex question of the future of Islam is very closely related to its relationship with Western civilization as it is the Western civilization that is triumphant today and is in a position to decide what space will be, or will not be, granted to Islam in the modern world. It is, therefore, pertinent to take a quick look at the nature of Western civilization so as to judge how far its pressure over Islam to trim itself in consonance with modern Western ideals could help the situation.

It is evident now that in the pursuit of material progress Western civilization has lost sight of the inherent nature of humankind. It wrongly holds that material affluence

---

[120] Allawi, p. 169.

can bless humans with true happiness and contentment. The fact remains, however, that while a human is a physical self, he is also a mind, a heart and a soul, each of which urges for gratification in its own right. He also has conscience which differentiates between good and bad and demands moral justification for behavior. And, above all, God is man's need, greater than all other needs of his life: a human is a creation and is by nature incomplete unless and until he connects to his creator. Modern Western civilization has turned its face against all these realities and pushed them to a corner as "personal matters." The result is a moral chaos and spiritual depravation that have made the contemporary human truly miserable. Dwight D. Eisenhower, former president of the USA, makes a very revealing comment on this situation:

> Our affluent society rests on shaky moral grounds. We reach the moon and pollute the earth. We long for peace and go to war. An age that has split the atom must heal the splits in humanity.... If we each listen to the still small voice of conscience, we shall soon perceive that simple basic things, like goodness, purity, unselfishness, love, integrity, are our greatest and most priceless treasure. Seek affluence in these and the tragedies of misused material affluence will end in happiness for all.[121]

---

[121] Dwight D. Eisenhower (former US president), quoted by Lari, p. 50.

Modern Western civilization, in its zeal to build the grandest technological structure to ensure comfortable and luxurious living on earth, has erected high walls of cement and concrete which instill in humans a feeling of awe and inferiority. The undue importance that this structure has attained demands from man that he work day and night to maintain it. "Development" has now attained the status of the master and reduced "man" to the level of the attendant. Dr. Alexis Carrel comments: "Man should be the measure of all. On the contrary, he is a stranger in the world he has created…. Thus the enormous advance gained by the sciences of inanimate matter over those of living things is one of the greatest catastrophes ever suffered by humanity…. We are unhappy. We degenerate morally and mentally."[122]

Modern Western civilization is blindly running after "progress," disregarding the fact that by destroying the moral and spiritual fabric of the society, it now threatens man's essential "human" identity. If, for example, the "artificial intelligence" makes headway, who would save humans from becoming slaves to their machine-masters? And can we deny the possibility of the appearance of the "superhumans" who are potentially ready to force their way to take over modern civilization? Stephen Hawking, the greatest theoretical physicist of the twenty-first century, predicted in his last days

---

[122] Alexis Carrel, *Man the Unknown* (Mumbai: Wilco Publishing House, 20160), pp. 38-39.

that a race of "superhumans" could come into existence as a result of genetic engineering which would be far more superior in physical and intellectual powers to normal human beings and "could destroy humanity" or enslave it.[123] And how much is our good earth safe in the presence of the weapons of mass destruction which could destroy this universe several times with its present stock? What happens if, God forbid, the Third World War erupts? Granted, civilizational common sense and humanitarian judiciousness would not let anything like this happen, but then, didn't the Second World War take place in spite of the fact that humans had the horrible experiences of the First World War fresh in mind? Why do the superpowers insist on producing, "improving" and trading in the world market weapons of mass destruction? Who in the world really needs these weapons and how can these weapons of mass destruction improve the quality of life on earth?

4. WHERE DOES THE FUTURE LIE?

Modern civilization has changed the world into a global village, but it has not been able so far to transform its residents into a

---

[123] Press Trust of India, London, *Indian Express,* "Stephen Hawking had warned against 'superhumans,' Monday, 15 October, 2018, page 9.

global family. Efforts are being made in order to eliminate divisions, but the chasm is widening at all levels. It seems that the present materialist civilization, which naturally creates greed for a larger share in each partner, cannot justly safeguard the interests of the privileged and the unprivileged alike. A stronger player like Religion is needed to redress the situation. Religion, all religions, must be given a chance to contribute. Islam with its comprehensive teachings and practical world view has a strong claim that it could lead humanity out of this chaos. Arnold Toynbee analyzes the present-day crisis and comes to the same conclusion. He says:

> The future lies with whatever religion or religions can create the spiritual brotherhood that is mankind's need today. Communism claims to be a sovereign unifier: Islam has been proving itself to be a unifier in Africa: Christianity could play the same role if it could bring itself to live up to its principles.[124]

5. LET THE TWAIN MEET

It is the need of the time that modern Western civilization reconsider its goals. It should communicate with Religion and benefit from its rich moral and spiritual experiences. It should especially eliminate its prejudice against Islam and check how

---

[124] Arnold Toynbee, "Islam: the Future Wave of the World," in *The Islamic Review*, March 1961, p. 3.

Islam could help in the formation of a new world order apt to make man duty-oriented and human-friendly.

Muslims, in their turn, should also assure the West (and its allies) that Islam's cherished goal is to help humanity break the shackles of coercion and exploitation and let humans live in freedom and dignity. On a historic occasion the Caliph Omar had rebuked the governor of Egypt whose son had unjustly whipped a Coptic Christian by saying, "Since when have you started enslaving a human being whom his mother had given birth as free?" Muslims should convince the West that, in fact, the cherished objective of the West and Islam at this point is one and the same.

If the West and Islam shed their suspicions against each other and contribute together to the formation of a global family which is blessed with material affluence, moral enlightenment and spiritual contentment, it will be a service to mankind that it needs most today. As Toynbee writes: "In the Atomic Age we have to choose between two extremes. If we are not to destroy ourselves, we have to learn to live as a single united human family embracing all mankind without exception."[125]

---

[125] Toynbee, p. 4.

Bibliography

English

Ahmad, Ziauddin, *Influence of Islam on World Civilization,* New Delhi, Adam Publishers and Distributers, 2006.

Ali, Ameer Syed, *The Spirit of Islam*, Calcutta, S. K. Lahiri & Co., 1902.

Allawi, Ali A., *The Crisis of Islamic Civilization*, London, Yale University Press, 2009.

Arnold Sir Thomas and Guillaume, Alfred, *The Legacy of Islam,* New Delhi, Kitab Bhavan, 2009.

Bodley, R. C., *The Messenger: The Life of Muhammad*, New York, Doubleday & Co., 1946.

Briffault, Robert, *The Making of Humanity,* London: George Allen & Unwin, 1919.

Carrel, Alexis, *Man the Unknown,* Mumbai: Wilco, 2016.

Esposito, John H. *The Future of Islam*, New York, Oxford University Press, 2010.

Fuller, Graham E. *A World without Islam,* New York: Back Bay Books: Little, Brown and Company, 2010).

Hitti, philip K., *The Arabs: A Short History,* Washington, D. C. , Regency Publishing, 1996.

Lari, Sayyed Mujtaba Musavi, *Western Civilization Through Muslim Eyes*, transl. by F. J Gouling, Qom, Foundation of Islamic C. P. W, 2008.

M. Basharat Ali, "Contribution of Muslims in the Field of Sociology," in *Muslim Contribution to Science*, by Mirza and Siddiqui (details below).

Meyerhof, Max, "Science and Medicine," in *Legacy of Islam,* by Arnold Sir Alfred Thomas and Guillaume, New Delhi, Kitab Bhavan, 2009.

Mirza, Md. R. and Siddiqui, Mohd. Iqbal, *Muslim Contribution to Science*, New Delhi, Adam Publishers, 2005.

RamaKrishna, Rao K. S., *Muhammad: the Prophet of Islam*, New Delhi, Madhur Sandesh Sangam, 2016.

Vaux, Carra de, "Astronomy and Mathematics," in *Legacy of Islam,* by Alfred Arnold Sir Thomas and Guillaume, New Delhi, Kitab Bhavan, 2009.

Wallace-Murphy, Tim, *What Islam Did for Us*, London, Watkins Publishing (first South Asian Edition), 2008.

Watt, Montgomery W., *The Majesty That Was Islam*, London, Sidgwick & Jackson, 1984.

Urdu

Briffaul, Robert, *Tashkeele Insaniyat* (trans. of *The Making of Humanity*, by Abdul Majid Salik), Lahore, Majlise Taraqqiye Adab, 1994, (via Marfat.com).

Nadwi, Sayyid Abul Hasan Ali, *Muslim Mamaalik men Islamiyat awr Maghribiyat ki Kashmakash*, Lucknow, Majlise Tahqiqaato Nashriyaat, 2011.

............, *Seerate Rasoole Akram*, Dare Arafaat, Rae-Bareili, Sayyid Ahmad Shaheed Academy, 2005.

Nadwi, Shah Moinuddin, *Siyarus Sahabah*, vol. 1, (Lahore: Idara Islamiyaat, n.y),

Sharqawi, Mohammad Ali, *Aalami Tahzibo Thiqafat par Islam ke athraat*, transl. Suhayb Alam and Najmus Sehar, New Delhi, Al-Balagh Publications, 2007.

Siddiqui, Mahmudul Hasan and Hasrat, Chiragh Hasan, *Taarikhe Islam*, New York: Silver Burdett Co., 1953.

Index